Introduction

A compass reliably points to the north. It is a practical aid for those who are lost. A moral compass points to human fulfillment and is of great help to those who are confused. A compass, of course, is a mechanism. Therefore, it is free from any ambiguities. A moral compass, by contrast, does not work on its own. Its possessor is a human being who is free to utilize it or disregard it. We all possess a moral compass whether we use it or not. All we need to activate our moral compass is to put into play certain factors, called "pointers" that direct us out from the wilderness of confusion into the broad daylight of reality within which self-realization becomes more readily attainable.

This book is intended to be of assistance to anyone who is confused about life. It makes reference to 25 pointers, all of which direct a person to a more complete realization of his personhood. These pointers stress the importance of order, nature, virtue, philosophy, justice, truth, harmony, and so forth.

It is my genuine hope that the reader will profit in some way from reading this book.

Dr. Donald DeMarco
February 22, 2020
Kitchener, Ontario

The Importance of Order

Benjamin Franklin, among his numerous contributions to civilization, bequeathed to the world a stream of deathless aphorisms: A penny saved is a penny earned; time lost is never found again; nothing is certain save death and taxes; there was never a good war, or a bad peace; honesty is the best policy. And if so many of his aphorisms are nothing but platitudes, he redeems himself by stating, "Be at war with your vices, at peace with your neighbors, and let every New Year find you a better man".

My favorite of his timeless proverbs, for purely philosophical reasons, is his statement that there is "A place for everything, everything in its place". It is a practical bromide indicating that everything should be stored someplace and when not in use should be returned to its proper place. I put my socks in a particular draw and put them back in that same drawer when they return from the laundry. This simplifies life and enables us to know where things are when we want to use them. Without such order, life would quickly degenerate into chaos: "Where are my socks? Must I go to work barefooted?" Misplacing our car keys or credit card can be calamitous. Misplacement is a sin against order. Nonetheless, the missing items must be somewhere, even if they are not in the right place. We must engage in a search to relocate them

All this is nothing but common sense, and the author of *Poor Richard's Almanack* was, indeed, a man of uncommon common sense. However, this practical bromide does not work for philosophy. If we misplace an idea, a strange thing happens - - it disappears. A more profound aphorism, an axiom, rather, is that it belongs to the wise man to order (*Sapientis est ordinare*). This ordering has a specific and time honored meaning. It refers to putting philosophical ideas or values in their proper ordering. God comes first and His creatures come second. When we place the creature ahead of God we can no longer find God - - He disappears.

We know that in getting dressed, we must put our socks on *before* we don our shoes. The contrary, if it could be carried out, would be *preposterous*. This is a wonderfully philosophical word for it means that if we put first (*pre-*) what should be second (*posterius*), we have done something foolish, or *preposterous*. It is *preposterous*, then, to put God ahead of man.

The sanctity of life should precede how we respond to life. It should come first. Now, if we place convenience before the sanctity of life, we run the danger of losing sight of the sanctity of life. When the proper order is breached, what should be primary disappears. The abortion issue, for example is a question of order. To the pro-abortionist, who places convenience or some other secondary factor first, he becomes an agnostic, so to speak, with regard to the sanctity of life. Since it has disappeared from his plane of thought, he believes that it does not exist. Therefore, he maintains that pro-life people believe in something that does not exist. Under such circumstances, a debate is not possible. If unicorns do not exist, there is no reason to discuss them as if they did exist.

In his discussion on the "sanctity of life" (*Foreign Policy*, September/October 2015), bioethicist Peter Singer has this to say: "During the next 35 years, the traditional view of the sanctity of human life will collapse under pressure from scientific, technological, and demographic developments. By 2040, it may be that only a rump of hard-core, know-nothing religious fundamentalists will defend the view that every human life, from conception to death, is sacrosanct".

Nothing could be clearer. For Professor Singer, once the sanctity of life has lost its primacy, it simply vanishes. Its lingering adherents, then, must be regarded as old fogies or fools. Debate is not possible.

Concerning marriage, to take another example. The unbreakable knot of love and an openness to children comes first. Everything else in its proper ordering comes after that. But if marriage is considered a mere practical arrangement that serves the practical interests of the spouses, the pre-eminence of love and openness to procreation is in danger of disappearing. Once it disappears, it cannot be relocated and its supporter appear to be atavistic or even ridiculous.

We should look before we leap, think before we act, discern before we choose, and disregard the Nike commercial that tells us, "Just do it". In the grand order of things, the spiritual must precede the material. There is no clearer violation of this principle than during the Christmas season when commercialism so often eclipses the spiritual significance of the Nativity. Politicians promise material progress and are silent about spiritual values. "Nothing will ever be reformed in this age or country," wrote G. K. Chesterton, "unless we realize that the moral fact comes first". When the material order takes precedence, the spiritual order vanishes and is nowhere to be found.

A moral value must be assigned to its proper place so that we can know where it is in relation to the proper place of other moral values. Thus, truth must be placed before justice. Without this progression, truth disappears and justice is downgraded into license. Similarly, justice must precede mercy, otherwise mercy is nothing more than a sentimental indulgence. Philosophy insists that each value be given its proper place so that the sequence of order with regard to other values corresponds to the wisdom of the wise man. The contrary proves disastrous: moral values disappear and we are left with a disorder that puts our own lives in disorder.

The Reality of God

The term "atheism" is very broad and not confined to a simple disbelief in God. Jacques Maritain, in his book, *The Range of Reason*, develops three types of atheism. These three types, although distinctive in their own way, are not entirely separated from each other. They represent a truly dynamic trio.

In the first kind, we find by far its largest membership. Maritain calls it "practical atheism". It is witnessed by people who profess a belief in God, but live as though God does not exist. The mere assertion that one is not an atheist does not exclude him from being identified by that term. A true belief in God demands a life that should reflect that belief. The practical atheist lives as if he were an atheist, his posturing notwithstanding. The Gospel denounces such people as "whited sepulchers".

The second kind of atheism for Maritain is the person who claims to have found God. But the god he honors is not the true God. Maritain calls these people "pseudo-atheists" because they believe in a false god. These false gods are in abundant supply in the modern world. For Jean-Paul Sartre it is absolute freedom; for Karl Marx it is the dialectic of history; for Friedrich Nietzsche it is the super-man (*ubermensch*); for Auguste Comte it is Humanity; for secular feminism it is autonomy. These gods, whom Ignatio Silone, in this anthology on the subject, has referred to as "the gods who failed," are abstractions and infinitely removed from God the Creator of heaven and earth. As abstractions, they can confer no benefit upon mankind. In fact, because of their essential unreality, the can be extremely harmful.

The third kind of atheist is the out-and-out variety, one who utterly denies the existence of God, even the false gods. These are, in Maritain's terminology, the "absolute atheists". In this case, they are more "anti-theists" than "atheists". Nonetheless, as Maritain contends, "absolute atheism" is really a form of religion. Maritain refers to it as "an act of faith in reverse gear". This type of atheist, strangely enough, disbelieves in God as ardently as a faithful Christian believes in Him. The true Christian is well advised to be an "atheist" with regard to the false gods. As St. Justin once remarked, "We are called atheists. And yes we confess it, we are atheists of those so-called gods".

How are die-hard atheists formed? Maritain's answer to this question sheds a great deal of light on the contemporary situation, perhaps even more so that it did in 1942 when he formulated his thoughts about atheism. The hypocrisy of the practical atheist serves as a scandal to others. It tends to generate a belief in a false god who will bring about some kind of utopia on earth, or an unlimited freedom that results from a complete rejection of God. In sum, a bad Catholic, for example, can contribute to the formation of a committed atheist, and yet, absolute atheism degenerates into a contradiction. As Maritain notes, atheism "proclaims that all religion must necessarily vanish away, and it is itself a religious phenomenon". Thus, the failure of Catholics to witness God in their lives can lead to a form of atheism in which people reject God in their lives. This occurrence may be correlated with the "butterfly effect" in which something virtually unnoticed and seemingly innocent can produce surprising and possibly deleterious effects.

If one does not see God reflected in the life of a Christian, a plausible conclusion is that the Christian is either delusional or that there is no God. One of the roots of atheism, therefore, is the Christian whose only connection with God is verbal. This stance impresses no one.

Maritain does not see atheism as just another viewpoint to be respected along with every other viewpoint concerning God's existence or non-existence. His thought on the matter is the perfect antithesis of religious indifferentism. In one way or another, for Maritain, atheism is at the root of all the evils that beset the world today. The "Peasant of the Garonne" is most emphatic on this point: "Under penalty of death civilization will have to overcome atheism and free itself of its inspiration". In no way are theism and atheism equal. As St. Paul has stated, "Light and darkness have nothing in common". Sightedness and blindness differ as perfection does to deprivation.

An analogy may serve to further clarify the dynamic interplay involved in the three kinds of atheism. Let us recognize three kinds of people who have failed to find love. In the first case, a person, quite simply, has not found love. The root of his problem, most likely, is that he is *self-centered*. He has failed to locate love in any objective sense. A second type believes he has found love, but has wrongly associated it with pleasure, or some other form of ego-satisfaction. Here, a false love is identified as love. Such a person is *confused*. In the third instance, a person may despair in searching for love and come to the conclusion that love does not exist. This is the profile of one who is *cynical*.

It should be easy to understand how not finding love and wrongly identifying it can lead to a despair about the very existence of love. The first two are stepping stones to the third, just as the first two forms of atheism are pathways toward absolute atheism.

People influence each other, whether they realize it or not, in many important ways. The love of God, witnessed in a person's daily life, is not only an affirmation of love, but a validation of God's existence. It is, therefore, a preventative of both cynicism and absolute atheism.

The Universality of Music

Four musical themes are swirling around in my head. They are events, more than musical performances, and are rich in metaphysical significance. These events involve the integration of musical compositions, its performers and the audience. Music cannot exist by itself. In order to be complete, it requires the addition of an interpreter and a listener. Nor could heaven exist without Love, loving, and loved ones.

The first involves eighty-eight-year-old Arthur Rubinstein performing the second movement of Chopin's second piano concerto which the composer wrote when he was nineteen. An octogenarian playing the music of a teenager (1975)! And yet, there was a perfect symbiosis that received rave reviews. Rubinstein, by his own admission, came to a fuller understanding of Chopin's music in his later years. It is most extraordinary, then, for a teenager to compose music of lasting and universal significance that requires one of the most insightful concert pianists in the world a virtual lifetime to comprehend it to his satisfaction?

The second involves concert pianist Vladimir Ashkenazy entertaining fellow pianist Nobuyuki Tsjii at his former home in Iceland and asking his protégé to play a few chords in the piano. Tsjii more than obliged by playing the opening movement of Chopin's first piano concerto. Ashkenazy was born in Russia and Tsjii in Japan. Ashkenazy (age 81) married an Icelandic pianist whose father was a symphony conductor. Tsjii (age 30) was born blind and yet shared the gold prize in the 2009 Van Cliburn International Piano competition. In this scenario, music had obliterated the- distances between Russia, Japan, Iceland, and Poland. Good music has nothing to do with geography, though throughout history, geography has been a constant occasion for war.

The third involves Jehudi Menuhin who, at twelve years of age, and on the night of April 4, 1929 in Berlin, Germany, performed the Bach, Beethoven and Brahms violin concertos. To have played all three of these demanding works at such a tender age and in a single night is more than remarkable; it borders on the supernatural. Menuhin is Jewish. The three composers are Christian, although belonging to different denominations. As duly reported in *The New York Times*, none other than Albert Einstein, a Jew whose religion faith resembles that of Spinoza, rushed from his seat in the audience to the dressing room where his lifted the young lad and said: "Today, Yehudi, you have once again proved to me that there is a God in heaven".

The fourth is borrowed from the Stephen King classic, *Shawshank Redemption* (1994). Tim Robbins' character uses his privileged position with the prison governor to broadcast over the tannoy system, a recording of *Duettino sull'aria* (a little duet on the breeze) from Mozart's *The Marriage of Figaro.* Prisoners stopped what they were doing. They were transfixed, in awe of this completely unexpected and beautiful gift. Two female vocalists were expressing in music something from another realm. In the motion picture version, the honey-toned voice-over of Morgan Freeman says to the audience: "I'd like to think they were singing about something so beautiful it can't be expressed in words and makes your heart ache because of it".

These four musical themes tell us in a most striking way that music transcends age, geography, religion, and occupation. We might add *time* since Johan Sebastian Bach was born in 1685. Music is universal in the sense that it has the power to unite all members of the human race. As a form of beauty, it is the seamless integration of truth and goodness. It is not truth in the abstract nor goodness as mere pleasure. It compels the whole person and makes him aware of a higher world where the brotherhood of mankind is not divided by the arrogance of the individual.

The Humanity of Justice

I did not deliver the following lecture, though I have given talks to law students. The following is based on a rather vivid dream I had. The essential idea in the dream seemed to have sufficient merit to be transcribed into a written article.

Good morning! I am most honored and pleased to have the opportunity to speak to you and I address you as future lawyers, judges, and perhaps even members of the Supreme Court. The future often brings more than we could have hoped for.

As I mounted the steps of this hallowed hall, the largest on the campus of the North American Institute for the Study of Criminal Law, what impressed me was how much has gone into preparing you to serve the interests of law. I was told that this particular building cost 4½ million dollars and it took 5 years to construct. Paintings of distinguished jurists grace your hallways. Your faculty represents a fine assemblage of instructors who have been carefully trained over many years to provide you with the education you need in order to be successful in your careers. You must be doing something very important to justify the expense and human sacrifice that has gone into your training.

But today, I want to begin by saying something that you may not have thought about, something which is paradoxical, extraordinary, and, in as sense, truly amazing. I want to allude to the simple factor that has given rise to the vast multitude of factors that are now an essential part of your life. The human organism, as we know from science, begins with a one-celled zygote and grows to an adult composed of roughly 35 trillion integrated cells. I recall, while in Minnesota, being captivated by the origin of the Mississippi River. What starts out as a stream, virtually a trickle, becomes, when it arrives at the delta in New Orleans, a mighty waterway. Small beginnings can produce stupendous results.

Now I ask, what is the seed, the humble beginning from which the gigantic apparatus of this school of criminal law develops? I will write two words on the blackboard and ask you to think about how they relate to each other. Here are the words: "accusation" and "conviction". If a conviction rested solely on an accusation, life would be simple and there would be no need for a law school and the million things that goes with it. If I accuse you of stealing my watch, you are thereby convicted of theft and there is no need for some kind of due process. The cold fact that you did not pilfer my watch is entirely irrelevant. The most heartbreaking book I have ever read is *The Ox-Bow Incident* by Zane Grey. In the story, two men are accused of murder and, without any supporting evidence, are executed. One of the victims is allowed time to write a letter to his wife, professing his love for her and insisting on his innocence. It was later revealed that the two men were innocent.

I was enraged by the story. Something crucial was missing, something that made it all too clear that a mere accusation is not the same as a conviction. That something, of course, is justice. And because we love justice, we go to elaborate means to help ensure that it prevails. We educate and train people such as yourselves to go through endless inconveniences to prove to the world that a conviction must be just and not merely the product of an accusation.

And so, we are all terribly inconvenienced because we must take the difficult road and make sure that justice, not accusation, determines guilt or innocence. There is an old adage that justice is "what the judge ate for breakfast". There are more jokes about the law profession than about any other profession. Perhaps this is because the law poses ideals that are so difficult to realize. The kindest quip I have ever come across is that lawyers do not grow old, they just lose their appeal.

To make my point using two different words, let me salute you as "executives" and not as "executioners". The executioner takes the easy way out. His main concern is power, not justice. Let us not follow in the footsteps of King Henry VIII who executed not only some of his best friends, but two of his own wives. The inclusion of justice makes things more difficult, but it also makes things more beautiful, and all beautiful things are the result of surmounting difficulties. It also makes thing more human, and human beings are who we all are. We abandon our humanity at our own peril.

Former Connecticut Senator Thomas Dodd, who must have said wiser things, once remarked that "There ought to be a law so a man knows whether he is doing right or wrong". Things cannot be that simple. In the final analysis it is not the law that determines justice, but justice that determines the law. And the law must rest on truth. The word "verdict" (*verum* + *dicere*) means to tell the truth.

As future ambassadors of the law, you must be devoted to justice and truth, values that are not always easy to come by. In addition, you need the courage to stand up for justice and truth. What went into the very building we are now occupying in terms of time and energy is prototypic of your own formation. Character that is woven of courage, justice and truth requires time, but its flower is of inestimable significance to the world. I recall a *bon mot* of G. K. Chesterton who said, "If seeds in the black earth can turn into such beautiful roses, what might not the heart of man become in its long journey toward the stars"?

May God bless you and always be at your side.

The Strength of Intelligence

Imagine a small spheroid—a baseball—travelling through the air. A group of scientists study it carefully and determine its velocity, its spin rate, its wind resistance, and it deviations along its trajectory. They do this with scientific precision and are prepared to tell the world all about the whirling adventures of this flying orb.

But what they cannot determine, given their limited field of study, is the baseball's efficient and final causes. The thin slice of reality they examine is too small for such determinations. Herein lies a problem for scientists. They can examine what the can see and measure, but the purpose of the flight of the baseball remains hidden from them.

If scientists could enlarge their domain of investigation, they would realize that the pitcher hurled the spheroid toward a batter. A dual purpose is involved here: the pitcher intends to get the batter out, while the batter intends to get on base. Let us now consider Chris Sale of the Boston Red Sox pitching to Manny Machado of the Los Angeles Dodgers. He throws a nasty slider and strikes out his opponent. At this moment a multiplicity of purposes come into play. The pitch is a strike; it is strike three; it is the final out of the game; it is victory for Boston; and it concludes the 2018 World Series. All these purposes are evident to the baseball fan, although not to the empirical scientist.

Taylor Caldwell, in her 1967 novel, *Dialogues with the Devil*, has a group of highly trained atheistic scientists locked in a room for all eternity studying what their instruments can reveal to them. They have at their disposal every tool of scientific inquiry as well as every reference book. Their life, however, is an icon of unrelieved frustration since the purpose of their work forever eludes them. We are purpose-oriented beings by nature. Without purpose there is no meaning. And we cannot tolerate a meaningless existence. Science cannot reveal to us either the purpose or the meaning of life.

Sir Isaac Newton expressed the limitations of scientific investigation when he likened himself to a small boy playing at the seashore diverting himself by finding a smoother pebble here or a prettier shell there, "while the great ocean of truth lay all undiscovered before me". More than a quarter of a millennium has passed from the birth of Sir Isaac Newton (1642) to the birth of Werner Heisenberg (1901). Yet their philosophies are quite similar. "The first cup of natural science makes you an atheist," Heisenberg once remarked, "But at the bottom of the cup, God is waiting".

The *Book of Proverbs* made this known to mankind long before the arrival of these two great physicists": "Many are the plans in the mind of man, but it is the purpose of the Lord that will be established" (19:21).

Science does not disclose purpose. We need to go beyond the mere motions of matter in order to grasp the purpose that lies beyond the facts. Yet so many scientists insist that purpose is not only undiscoverable but non-existent. In his book, *River Out of Eden*, Richard Dawkins states that "The Universe we observe has precisely the properties we should expect if there is, at bottom, no design, no purpose, no evil and no good, nothing but blind and pitiless indifference" (p. 133).

We should ask Mr. Dawkins to take a more careful look. The single-cell zygote is no larger than a grain of sugar. Nonetheless, it initiates a development that progresses to form the 30-trillion- cell highly unified organism that is the human adult. The human infant produces 200 neurons in his brain per minute. This prodigious rate slows down a bit until it forms the adult brain which consists of roughly 100 billion neurons. Here we find a pattern of organization—design, that is—which is more highly integrated than anything that is man-made. The Taj Mahal, for example, is less complex and has less organization that any one of the architects that planned it. To cite Newton once again, "Gravity may put the planets into motion, but without the divine Power, it could never put them into such a circulating motion as they have about the Sun; and therefore, for this as well as other reasons, I am compelled to ascribe the frame of this System to an intelligent Agent".

We human beings are the beneficiaries of God's purpose. We were meant to be. We might say that God threw out the first pitch. This brings to mind the ceiling of Michelangelo's Sistine Chapel that depicts an eager God-the-Father reaching out to a reluctant Adam. God may throw out the first pitch, but man is not always willing to catch it. God has granted us our existence. But far more than that, he has given us a home. Gerard Verschuuren, in his recent book, *In the Beginning: a Catholic Scientist Explains How God Made Earth Our Home*, comes to the conclusion that "The earth was made for us. Everything was indeed fine-tuned for our coming. We live in a purpose-driven universe. Gone are chaos, mere randomness, and utter purposelessness".

In addition, we can say that our home is fully furnished. We have light and warmth from the sun, and at our disposal are the means for providing food, clothing, and shelter. We find the beauty of nature, and are inclined to seek truth and live a good life. We are equipped with minds that seek knowledge through science, hearts that express themselves in art, and souls that search for wisdom through philosophy and theology. We are not one-dimensional. We are not mere scientists. Our home is not the laboratory, but a fully furnished universe.

The Blessing of Communion

Virtually every form of sex education commits the same mistake. This mistake has to do with positioning sex in the wrong place. Order is paramount. In relating to human beings, humanness comes first, one's sexual identity (male or female) comes second. The expression "sex education" is a misnomer because it gives primacy to sex whereas the primacy belongs to one's humanity.

Scripture is clear on this point. Prior to meeting Eve, Adam was preoccupied with plants and animals. He was familiar with many species of life but did not know anyone who belonged to his own species. In his "Theology of the Body" John Paul II described Adam's condition as "cosmic solitude". This solitude was needed, however, in order for Adam to appreciate fully his human counterpart when she finally arrived.

Before Eve was created, God put Adam into a deep sleep (*Tardemah* in Hebrew). The special meaning assigned to this word indicates that God alone was involved in the creation of the first woman. Thus, Eve was a gift. The notion of gift carries with it gratitude toward the giver and the proper care of the gift. Adam must respect Eve since she is a special gift from God.

In *Genesis* 2:24 we are told how Adam initially responds to this gift: "This at last in bone of my bones and flesh of my flesh". Adam regards the woman primarily as another human being, one that he longed for with all his heart. Since Eve was formed from Adam's side, she is his equal in humanity. Scripture does not indicate the moment at which Adam perceived Eve as his sexual complementary. We are told, however, that they married and had children.

Adam is a role model for all men. He sees the woman initially as a human being, and one who is a gift from God and his equal. This order is apparent when a woman gives birth to a child. She sees her child first as a human being, and also a gift who is equal in humanity with regard to the human family. Upon delivery, the doctor may announce that the child is a boy or a girl. The more proper expression "relationship education" should replace the misleading phrase "sex education".

After sinning against God, Adam and Eve lost sight of this original order. At this point, co-humanity was wrenched from its proper place, an experience which cause shame and prompted the couple to cover themselves with fig leaves. This fall from grace emphasized all the more how the proper order moving from humanity to sexuality is fundamental.

The literal meaning of the Hebrew term, "Teshuvah" is "return" and refers to repentance. To sin is to get things out of order. Repentance means getting back to the right order. Christ came into the world for the purpose of restoring order. In the realm of human sexuality this means putting sex in the right place and not allowing it to obscure one's humanity. If a batter hits the ball and runs directly to second base, he is declared out. He must abide by the rules of the game. First base comes first. No other arrangement is tolerated.

It is all too common for men (and women as well) to see their sexual complement primarily as sexual. The fact that men can behave as wolves and women as vixens is a strong indication that in losing sight of another's humanity, one loses sight of his own and begins to resemble a beast. The way human beings retain their operative humanity is to greet the other primarily as human beings. The "playboy-playmate" arrangement is not liberation but dehumanization.

Enlarging upon this notion, we can say that in the proper ordering of things friendship takes precedence over a sexual relationship, the former serving as a basis and guide for the latter. By placing sex first, friendship is over-ridden. Marriage requires a strong friendship. It cannot rest on sex alone. Marriage incorporates sex, but sex lacks the wherewithal to incorporate marriage. The sequence of sex, living together, unwanted offspring and abortion is clearly, no matter how common it is, not something to which people should be educated.

Personalist philosophers—Saint John Paul II, Jacques Maritain, Gabriel Marcel, Nikolai Berdyaev, Martin Buber, Soren Kierkegaard, etc.—stress the importance of "intersubjectivity". This word describes a person-to-person relationship that is primarily human. We are, to ourselves, subjects. We do not want others to regard us as objects; nor should we want to see them as objects. Love means breaking down the alienating walls of objectivity and seeing each one another as subjects. It means seeing each other as we are in our humanity.

Yet, we persist in avoiding the first step and regard the other, if not as primarily sexual, as primarily wealthy, good-looking, athletic, influential, and so on. Humanity, which is the basis of love, justice, and peace, gets lost in the shuffle and becomes difficult to rediscover. Secondary features should remain secondary.

Cardinal Newman's honored phrase, *cor ad cor loquitur* (heart speaking to heart) refers to what the personalist philosophers have in mind when they speak of "intersubjectivity". As human beings, we have hopes, dreams, disappointments, sufferings, longings, talents, and so forth. These factors constitute interesting dialogue on the purely human plane. When a patient arrives in the emergency room of a hospital, he is presented and treated primarily as a human being. Sex, race, ethnicity, social status, and religious belief, are not critical at that moment. The person's welfare as a human being is all that counts.

Relationship education is all about putting first things first. And when sex comes first, lust and mayhem are sure to follow. We should begin a relationship by acknowledging the other as a gift who is equal to us in humanity.

The Propriety of Rectitude

One of the most bizarre features of the modern world is that ad men and retailers try to make products out to be more than they are, while certain lawyers and philosophers are at pains to make human beings out to be less than they are. One has to fight against the current of culture in order to have a fighting chance to get things straight.

A "permanent" hair style is temporary; "Joy" does not make dishwashing a joyful experience; "5-Day Deodorant" does not last for five days; and a certain after shave lotion does not cause a bevy of adoring females to materialize out of thin air. We should remember that it is man who makes the clothes, and not the clothes that make the man.

The attempt on the part of some professionals to denigrate the human being warrants more detailed attention. There is an inexpressible richness to the nature of human beings that is difficult to see when he is viewed in terms of a series of levels. The first level has to do with individuality, something that human beings have in common with everything that exists. Trees, oceans, stars, monkeys, and mountains all have a certain individuality. And that is why we assign them names.

It would be a grave injustice to evaluate the human being as merely an individual. Nonetheless, throughout history, man has been looked upon as little more than a functional individual having no rights or a property to be possessed by another. Oliver Wendell Holmes has gone on record stating that "I see no reason for attributing to man a significance different from that which belongs to a baboon or a grain of sand" (2 *Holmes-Pollock Letters*, 1942, p. 252). The 1857 *Dred Scott* decision, for example, held that slaves were property rather than persons.

A human being is more than an individual by virtue of his membership in the human species. But species membership, for some philosophers, does not entitle man to a privileged status. In his book, *Practical Ethics*, Peter Singer argues that "Some members of other species are persons; some members of our own species are not". Therefore, he reasons, "killing, say a chimpanzee is worse than the killing of a gravely defective human who is not a person". For Singer and others, man does not necessarily rise from the level of individual to the level of person.

The United States Supreme Court, in 1973, ruled in *Roe v. Wade* and in *Doe v. Bolton* that the unborn child is not a person at any time before birth within the meaning of the Fourteenth Amendment. In the words of the Court, "the word 'person,' as used in the Fourteenth Amendment, does not include the unborn". It is supremely ironic that The Fourteenth Amendment, which was a reaction to the *Dred Scott* case, was enlisted to depersonalize the unborn. The understanding of the human being has, historically, been both inconsistent and contradictory.

Shakespeare puts into the mouth of Hamlet, a beautiful panegyric on the special place than man occupies in the cosmos. "How noble in reason," he states, underscoring the time-honored view that man is a rational animal, and as such, sets him apart from chimpanzees and baboons. Indeed, as Hamlet continues, he is the "paragon of animals". Only man among all the animals is religious, artistic, philosophical, and literary. Only man builds hospitals for the sick, provides food for the poor, education for the ignorant, and asylums for the mentally handicapped. Man is not merely one species among innumerable other species. He transcends them all. He is not circumscribed by his biological classification, *Homo sapiens.* He belongs to a higher level than his taxonomy indicates.

"In apprehension like a God," as Hamlet continues. Man can know truth, goodness, and justice. He can, as Aristotle remarked, "know all things". He is created in the image of God and is His special creation – "the beauty of the world". And finally, as Hamlet concludes, "the quintessence of dust". He is a unification of body and soul, the highest of all material creatures (*quinta + essentia*). That "fifth essence" was regarded by the ancients as imperishable. And he is immortal.

After delivering this lofty statement on man, Hamlet then states that "Man delights not me – nor woman neither (Act 2, scene 2). There is nothing wrong with Hamlet's assessment of the human being. But something is missing. He is strangely alienated from everything he admires. He remains incomplete. He has not reached that level which crowns his humanity. The factor that would make everything that he admires enjoyable is the missing ingredient. Hamlet pines because there is no love in his life.

Man exists as an individual, but a very special one. He is a member of a species, but the loftiest of Species. He is a person who is both unique and communal. He is a being endowed with rights. But this description does not take into consideration what a human being is supposed to do with his life. Unless he is doing what he is supposed to be doing, he remains incomplete. The core Christian message is that love is the very meaning of life. We are born to love and to be loved. And even those who are handicapped in their manner of expressing love, can be the recipients of love from others.

We do not expect lawyers and philosophers to grasp the full meaning of the human being. But we do hope that they would have a sense of its transcendence, that they would be open to further levels of its being. At the same time, we should become more humanized ourselves so that others will begin to understand the great value and dignity we all possess as human beings.

The Glory of Excellence

In sports, you either win or lose, but you cannot win unless you play the game. This axiom applies to life as well as to philosophy. One cannot succeed in life unless he puts aside the fear of failure and gets involved. Likewise, one cannot succeed in philosophy unless he sheds the fear of being wrong and commits himself to the pursuit of truth.

Philosopher/theologian Paul Tillich employs the word "neurosis" to anyone who is so fearful of losing that he loses all hope of winning. Speaking in a general way, he states that a neurosis is "a way of avoiding non-being by avoiding being". A person's fear of failing a job interview may cause him to avoid it. Fear of rejection can lead to avoiding a marriage proposal, a moral responsibility, or any number of challenges that life presents. The fear of failure can eliminate the possibility of success.

Sports can serve as an inspiration for everyone. It is a world in which the underdog is not necessarily a loser. The United States hockey team understood this when it defeated the highly- rated Russian contingent at the 1980 Winter Olympics in Lake Placid, the so-called "Miracle on Ice". The spectacle of a group of amateurs defeating professionals offers hope for anyone who has the courage to go against the odds. "Amateur", as the word indicates, refers to anyone who loves what he is doing. This attitude can put an amateur in a more favorable position than the professional whose chief concern may be monetary.

In the 1988 World Series, Kirk Gibson came to bat as a pinch hitter in the bottom of the ninth inning with the tying run on base and two men out. He was too banged up to start the game, suffering from two bad legs and a damaged left hand. Manager Tommy Lasorda was rolling the dice. On the mound was Dennis Eckersley, one of baseball's premier relief pitchers. The Oakland hurler would win both the American League's MVP and Cy Young awards in 1992. Over his 24-year career the Hall of Fame pitcher won 197 starts and earned 390 saves. It was one of the great mismatches of all time, and put Mr. Gibson clearly behind the eight-ball. The count went to 3 and 2. On the final pitch of the game, Gibson, who could barely walk, hit an Eckersley slider into the right field seats, earning a most dramatic 6-5 win for the Los Angeles Dodgers. Broadcaster Vin Scully capped the event by saying that "In a year that has been improbable, the impossible has happened". It was not "impossible," for it did happen. It only seemed that way. And that is one of the great joys of life.

Vince Lombardi, the Hall of Fame coach of the Green Bay Packers, whom ESPN has acclaimed "Coach of the Century," would rally his troops by quoting St. Paul who enjoined his disciples to "fight the good fight" (2 Timothy 4:7). "If we chase perfection," he would say, "we can catch excellence". His son, Vince Jr. learned a great deal about character from his dad. In his book, *What It Takes to Be #1*, he provides an apt summary of his father's moral philosophy: "We live in a time when authority is questioned, gratification is instant, morals are relative, ethics are situational, and the truth is apparently whatever we decide it is. We lead lives of comfort and ease and, as a result, we've lost our hunger to lead and achieve. Today, fewer people are willing to make the sacrifices that are necessary to become a leader."

The 'old college try' motto means that there is never a moment when a competitor should give up. He should never abandon effort even when losing appears to be imminent. He should always remain victorious in his spirit.

As a teacher of philosophy, I have encountered many examples, both in the classroom and in books, of people giving up on philosophy because they have come to think that truth is unattainable. The legacy of Pontius Pilate—"What is Truth"—continues unabated. Admittedly, the possession of truth, like any other victory, often requires overcoming certain obstacles. Cicero said long ago that there is no nonsense in the world which has not found some philosopher to maintain it. Surely, there are difficulties one encounters along the road to truth. Nevertheless, as philosopher Jacques Maritain avers, "it is the error of cowards to mistake a difficulty for an impossibility".

It is perfectly reasonable, then, to remind pro-lifers that they should never allow themselves to be discouraged, even when the odds seem to be stacked against them. Losing, in certain instances, may be inevitable, but not trying is unforgiveable. It is in the nature of the human being not to quit. We must never lose touch with that natural impulse.

The Nobility of Truth

All truths are interconnected, from the humblest to the holiest. I refer to the simplest of truths as those that can be answered by "yes" or "no". "Tell the truth, now, did you chop down that cherry tree?" George Washington's father asked his son. "Yes, I did; I cannot tell a lie," George replied. The truth of the matter was stated by the simple response of "yes". This affirmation represented the truth of what actually happened (at least in the tale told by Person Weems). A lie would have represented a non-reality, although a very small one. Truth is intimately connected with reality; the lie has no connection with reality. In this regard, Alexandr Solzhenitsyn's remark that "one word of truth outweighs the whole world" is itself true. The lie has no weight.

The "true or false" test operates on this same level. The answers are "right" or "wrong" according to whether they are "true" or "false". In the court of law a judge needs realistic evidence in order render a verdict. The word "verdict" is derived from two Latin words—*verum* and *dicere*—meaning, to tell the truth. There can be no justice without truth. The entire judicial system is dependent on man's ability to know the truth that will lead to a just verdict.

We can understand "truth" in a larger sense that can never be answered by a simple "yes". "What is man?" What is the meaning of life? What is God? There are no simple answers for such questions. People ascribe different answers to them. Some find them to be unanswerable conundrums. They are like the Riddle of the Sphinx, eternally evading the grasp of mortal man. To the ancient Greeks, the words "Know Thyself," inscribed in the forecourt of the Temple of Apollo at Delphi were placed there by the gods. So profound, they believed, was the truth about the human being.

"What is man that thou art mindful of him?" asks the Psalmist (8: 4-8). "O God," cried St. Augustine, "I pray you let me know myself." "Each of us is farthest away from himself," wrote Nietzsche, "as far as ourselves are concerned we are not knowers". The truth of the human being, critically important as it is, is mysterious and elusive. We are not simply angels or animals, merely individuals or part of the collective. We are complex, enigmatic, and ambiguous. "Homo duplex" was the name assigned to him by the medievalists.

How then, do we come to know who we are? In the second Vatican Council's Pastoral Constitution on "The Church in the world today," we read: "The fact is that only in the mystery of the incarnate Word is light shed on the mystery of man.

Adam, the first man, pre-figured the man to come, Christ the Lord, Christ is the new Adam, by revealing the mystery of the Father and his love, also fully reveals man to man himself and makes his exalted vocation known to him. It is therefore no wonder that all the truths set out above flow from Christ and reach their highest form of expression in him."

"I am the Way, the Truth, and the Life," Christ told us (*John* 14:16). This is an extraordinary statement. Whatever beams of illumination the Doctors of the Church proclaimed came from outside of them. They were not the source of Truth. But Christ *is* truth, the perfect integration of the ideal and the historical. And how important is the Truth that this personification of Truth makes available to us? "The truth will set you free" (*John* 8:32), he states, alluding to a Life that is free from sin and one that allows man to put himself on the Way back to God. There can be no real freedom without Truth. There can be no wholly authentic life without Truth.

God created man, but did not abandon him to his own devices. He provided a model to imitate. Jascha Heifetz is a model for violinists, as Arthur Rubinstein is for pianists. They reveal the truth, so to speak, of their art. They actualize the ideal. Christ is our model for life. He is to be imitated by anyone who wants to fulfill his being.

The simple truths that can be answered by a "yes" or a "no" are truths of fact. The truth of man is a truth of being and therefore more complex, richer, and profound. Before the truth of the human being, man is silent. The Truth that is Christ is a truth of being on a divine level.

The trial of Christ was a mockery of justice because it rejected both truth as well as Truth. It delivered not a true but a false verdict. It was not true that Christ was guilty. This was simply a matter of fact. But it also rejected Truth incarnate. Pilate's undying remark, "What is truth?" was a denial and rejection of truth on both of these levels. Here, we can see that even the small sin against truth can be interconnected with its largest transgression, the sin against God, one that Adam committed in the Garden of Eden. Had Pilate rendered a true verdict and held firmly to it, Christ would have been spared crucifixion. This total repudiation of truth paved the way for the greatest act of injustice the world has ever known - - the condemnation of God by man!

In his international best-seller, *Crossing the Threshold of Hope*, His Holiness John Paul II refers to Christ's trial as "that tragic proceeding in which man accused God before the tribunal of his own history, and in which the sentence handed down did not conform to the truth." We should not ask the question, "What is truth?" Rather, we should ask how best we can serve both truth and the Truth that is Christ.

The Benefits of the Intellect

Nature has equipped us with an autoimmune system of dazzling complexity and uncanny efficiency. It consists of 100 billion immunological regulatory receptors that are capable of distinguishing the self from the non-self. Its function is to protect the self from alien substances that are potentially harmful to it. No matter what the shape or form of the enemy invader, there will be some correlative receptor that can recognize it and effect its elimination.

Added to the wonder of how the autoimmune system recognizes self from non-self is its ability to distinguish between invading carbohydrates, nucleic acids, and proteins from those which exist within the organism, often in shapes that are exceedingly similar to those of the invaders. When the autoimmune system is functioning properly, it never gets activated by self-substances and unerringly responds to and rejects non-self-substances.

Whereas nature has endowed us with a splendid autoimmune system that takes care of the body, it is our responsibility to establish an intellectual immune system to protect us from accepting bad ideas. Dostoevsky spoke of how easily incomplete ideas that float on the wind can infect the minds of university students. He used this theme as the basis for his novel, *Crime and Punishment*. We need to protect ourselves from such half-baked ideas by installing a number of good ideas. Choice, for example, is an incomplete idea since it does not specific an object. Psychiatrist Viktor Franks has referred to a wrong set of ideas in culture as constituting a "psychic epidemic". Whereas somatic epidemics are typical results of war, he goes on to say, psychic epidemics associated with a virtual absence of a sound realistic philosophy of life are possible causes of war.

It is encouraging to note that although there are an infinite number of bad ideas, only a relatively few good ideas are needed to establish a reliable intellectual immune system. The operation is far less complicated and contains far fewer elements than what is required to create a fire wall to keep out computer viruses. A person does not need not know very much in order to be wise. The knowledge explosion need not be a source of confusion of discouragement for the person who wants to be properly educated in the fundamental sense of being able to distinguish between good and bad ideas. Philosophy, both speculative and practical, has made few if any advances in modern times. In this regards, there is hardly anything new under the sun. In fact, much has been lost as a result if errors that have infected modern thinking.

Education and a virtuous life are of critical importance. Philosopher and educator Mortimer Adler has written two books which marvellously illustrate the relatively uncomplicated way in which the mind can recognize error as such and reject it. The titles alone are instructive: *Six Great Ideas* and *Ten Philosophical Mistakes*. The former deals with Truth, Beauty and Goodness (ideas we judge by) and Liberty, Justice, and Equality (ideas we act on). The latter deals with 10 areas of thought that can protect us from commonly made errors. Dr. Adler's aim as an educator, indeed, is to help us to establish and strengthen our intellectual immune systems.

When we realize the importance of establishing a strong intellectual immune system, we realize, at the same time, the importance of philosophy. Philosophy as the pursuit of wisdom, it must be stated, is not to be placed alongside of trendy alternatives such as deconstructionism, relativism, scepticism, or cynicism. We need philosophy, not as an amusement, but in a fundamental way, the way the lungs need oxygen, the digestive system needs food, and the circulatory system needs blood.

According to St. Thomas Aquinas, we are inclined by nature to seek Truth, Beauty, Goodness, and so on. These inclinations are an elementary part of the Natural Law. Nature does not incline us to seek error. No one ever asks for the wrong time.

Every person wants to be an authentic "self," that is, a whole self both in body and soul. It should be noted, as scientists of immunology agree, that a healthy mind, consisting of good ideas, is a significant aid in strengthening the autoimmune system. Philosophy, then, is not only a pursuit of wisdom, but a path to fuller self-possession.

The Value of Variety

Canadian voters have re-elected Justin Trudeau as their Prime Minister. The October 21, 2019 election shows that the Liberal Party garnered 157 seats to 121 for the Conservatives. Four other parties gained 60 seats which means that a Liberal minority will be in power. The popular vote was much closer with the Conservatives getting 34.4% of the votes while the Liberals received 33.06%.

What is most striking about the election for this observer, living in Canada, is how so many Canadian voters seemed indifferent to the fact that their culture is clearly shifting in a totalitarian direction. A profile of the candidates is a sufficient indication of this. The Trudeau government required students applying for government funded summer jobs to sign an attestation professing their support of abortion, same-sex marriage and the LGBTQ coalition. He banned certain Christian summer camps from serving underprivileged children from participating in the Canada Summer Jobs Program because of their religious beliefs (This "is nothing short of anti-religious bigotry," commented Justice Centre staff lawyer Marty Moore). He has committed $7.1 billion over the next ten years to promote abortion at home and abroad. He will not allow Liberal MPs to vote their conscience on matters of abortion and LGBTQ matters, and will not allow pro-life candidates to run as Liberal candidates. He opposes conscience rights for health care workers.

Excepting Conservative candidate Andrew Scheer, the leaders of the New Democratic Party and the Green Party think the same way concerning abortion, same sex marriage, LGBTQ issues, doctor assisted suicide, and the decriminalizing of marijuana and prostitution. The NDP leader opposes conscience rights for health workers.

This promotion of a unanimity of thought together with an intolerance of dialogue has received considerable impetus from academe. In a university text book titled, *Sociology*, for example, Marlene Mackie of the University of Calgary states that "Canadian society could not continue to exist unless the thousands of new members born each year eventually learned to think, believe, and behave as Canadians. The continuity of our society requires that children come to embrace societal values as their own. Citizens must adhere to cultural norms because they themselves view those norms as right and proper". What this sociologist is really saying is that the aim of universities is to discourage students from thinking.

Michael O'Brien, in his 1993 booklet, *The Family and the New Totalitarianism"* warned his Canadian readers of a new form of totalitarianism that they might not recognize as such. The old totalitarianism conjured up in people's minds, he wrote, images of "barbed wire, jack-boots and thought-control". Most Canadians fail to see the new and oncoming totalitarianism because it is fed to them in the deceptive context of diversity and inclusivity. The watchdog is distracted by the bait and lets down his defenses.

What are the signs of totalitarianism? We may list seven: 1) unanimity of thought; 2) suppression of criticism; 3) denial of conscience; 4) abdication of reason; 5) government coercion; 6) mass conditioning of thought and will; 7) persecution of dissenters. All these signs are evident in Canadian society and they became crystal clear throughout the campaign. Omitted in all the discussion was the importance of spiritual values. In his book, *The Crisis of Western Education*, the eminent historian, Christopher Dawson, remarks that ignoring the "spiritual component in human nature and in the human psyche is a blunder so enormous that no advance in scientific method or educational technique is sufficient to compensate for it." The economy and scientific progress are unquestionably important, but they do not satisfy the essential needs of the human spirit.

"Unanimity of thought is the arteriosclerosis of society," said Anatole France. Dialogue, dealing with differences of opinion is required in a democratic society. Free citizens believe in the value of dialogue because they believe in the persuasive power of reason. Ideology smothers reason for the sake of a unanimity that is held together by power. Liberalism is not liberal when it attempts to force people into a mental straight jacket. As Christopher Dawson has stated in his book *Religion and the Modern State*, "Once society is launched on the path of secularization it cannot top at the half-way house of Liberalism; it must go on to the bitter end, whether that end is Communism or some alternative type of 'totalitarian' secularization."

Canadian "liberals" would do well to read Pope Benedict XVI's statement of *Truth and Tolerance*: "In all known historical cultures, religion is an essential element of culture, is indeed its determinative center; it is religion that determines the scale of values and, thereby, the inner cohesion and hierarchy of all these cultures". The Canadian election is much more significant than the election of certain individuals. It has been the election of untruth and intolerance.

The Merits of an Open Mind

Allan Bloom's 1987 best-seller, *The Closing of the American Mind*, shocked a great deal of readers by explaining why a university experience might not be an educational achievement. The author asserts that "There is one thing a professor can be absolutely certain of: almost every student entering the university believes, or says he believes, that truth is relative." The focus of education, Bloom observed, had drifted over the past half-century from a democratic society to a democratic personality. Hence, the jarring subtitle: "How Higher Education has Failed Democracy and Impoverished the Souls of Today's Students."

If we read the accounts written by Heather MacDonald, Ben Shapiro, Anthony Esolen, Jordan Peterson and others, we have reason to believe that university education has gotten much worse. Relativism at least recognizes that there are different values; it just does not know how to determine which ones are true. The closing of the American mind, however, has given way to dispensing with it altogether leaving students to operate on pure emotion.

Relativism was not an attack on university education as much as a modification of it. But its replacement—let us call it 'political correctness'--is not only an attack on education but a rejection of all of Western Civilization. It represents a retreat into a world of unbridled emotions for which there can be no rational antidote.

Heather MacDonald has produced a best-selling book on the current crisis in education: *The Diversity Delusion*: *How Race and Gender Pandering Corrupts the University and Undermines Our Culture*. In order to provide a striking contrast between old and new attitudes toward education, she presents two quotations. The first was written in 1903 by historian, philosopher and author W. E. B. DuBois: "I sit with Shakespeare and he winces not. Across the color line I move my arm in arm with Balzac and Dumas. I summon Aristotle and Aurelius and what soul I will, and they all come, all graciously with no scorn or condescension"

The contrasting quote is from a Columbia University student commenting on a music course: "Why do I have to listen to this Mozart? Who is this Mozart, this Haydn, these superior white men? There are no women, no people of color."

William Edward Burghardt DuBois (1868-1963) was the first African American to receive a doctorate from Harvard. He was a professor of Latin and Greek at Wilberforce University in Ohio. He taught other subjects at various other institutions. He wrote two novels, a book of essays and poetry, and other works. In 1919 he co-founded the National Association for the Advancement of Colored

People (NAACP). "Education," he remarked, "is that whole system of human training within and without the school house walls, which molds and develops men." Elsewhere he stated that "The function of the university is not simply to teach breadwinning, or to furnish teachers for the public schools, or to be a centre of polite society; it is, above all, to be the organ of that fine adjustment between real life and the growing knowledge of life, an adjustment which forms the secret of civilization."

DuBois has something to say to the current generation of university students. He would have heartily endorsed C. S. Lewis' advice of "keeping the clean sea breeze of the centuries blowing through our minds." But he is swept away because much of what he said belongs to a tradition that is now despised.

Shakespeare, Mozart, and the rest come to all of us without prejudice. We should be open to them in the same way that they are open to us. Why listen to Mozart? Why listen to any of the great black jazz pianists. Art Tatum performed for none other than Arthur Rubinstein, Vladimir Horowitz, and Sergei Rachmaninoff and won their highest praise. His playing was a melding of swing and classical music. He transformed several classical pieces, Dvorak's *Humoresque*, for example, into his own arrangements. Scott Joplin amalgamated African American songs with Western European music. If we should not listen to Mozart because he is white, why should we listen to the genius of Errol Garner, Duke Ellington, Count Basie, Earl Hines, Oscar Peterson, Mary Lou Williams, and countless others?

The root cause of the degeneration of university education is complex. Nevertheless, the decline of Christianity in American society has played a significant role. There are three points in Catholicism that are anathema to the secularist mind: 1) the reality of Original Sin; 2) the need for Divine Grace, 3) that this world is not our final destiny. The secular mind, not believing in an after-life, tries to create a paradise on earth. Secularists, therefore, refuse to believe that man is imperfect and can build a Utopia by himself. In this utterly impossible Utopia, no one would ever be offended. Therefore, all offenders must be dealt with swiftly and decisively. Even an innocuous question such as "Where do you come from" is categorized as a "micro-aggression" and must be avoided at all costs.

The word "Utopia," literally means "the place that is no place". Samuel Butler understood this which is why he titled his novel *"Erewhon,"* and imperfect anagram for the utopia that is "no where". With such strict and uncompromising rules, life becomes very difficult on today's college campuses. Students are reluctant to ask questions for fear they might violate the sacrosanct rules of political correctness". Similarly, teachers, especially those who lack tenure, are fearful of not toeing the line. Administrators worry about losing enrolment and troubling protests. Building a Utopia is serious business and no concessions should be made.

Unity is in truth. Without truth, distrust, dissension, and degeneration become inevitable. Truth is attainable, though it requires effort. This is why education is institutional and staffed by qualified personnel. We are presently confronted with a choice: education or barbarism.

The Power of Art

Francesco Rosario Capra, better known to fans of the cinema as Frank Capra, was born on May 18, (the birth date of Saint John Paul II) in Bisaquino, Sicily, the youngest of seven children. He died in La Quinta, California at the age of 94. The journey from Bisaquinto to La Quinta bears a curious literal resemblance to "Aquinas".

His family left for the United States in 1897 when Francesco was 5 years of age. As he recounted many years later in his autobiography, *The Name Above the Title*, it was the worst experience of his life, but seeing the statue of Liberty was the best experience of his life. This contrast between the worst and the best was to follow him throughout his life.

While in San Francisco, California, with twelve cents to his name, he answered a newspaper advertisement placed by an actor who was looking for a director to help him create film versions of his favorite poetry. He showed up at the studio, announced that he had just arrived from Hollywood, and fast-talked his way into his first directing role.

Capra did not always take his Catholic faith very seriously. He identified himself as a Christmas Catholic. He felt pretty good about himself when some of his earlier films were successes and, as a result, did not concern himself too much about his faith. A turning point in his life came when a friend said to him, "The talents you have, Mr. Capra, are not your own, not self-acquired. God gave you those talents; they are His gifts to you, to use for His purpose." Capra then re-evaluated his faith and began to take it more seriously. He began using his talents a new direction. "My films," he said, "must let every man, woman, and child know that God loves them, that I love them, and that peace and salvation will become a reality only when they all learn to love each other." In speaking about his film, *You Can't Take it With You*, Capra said that it was a chance to promulgate Christ's admonition to love thy neighbor which he averred "can be the most powerful sustaining force in someone's life".

In his 1971 autobiography he stated that "Mankind needed dramatizations of the truth that man is essentially good, a living atom of divinity; that compassion for others, friend or foe, is the noblest of all virtues. Films must be made to say these things, to counteract the violence and the meanness, to buy time to demobilize the hatreds." Hollywood moguls did not always agree with Capra's moral vision. "Capricorn" was the derisive label they ascribed to his movies. But his movies were hardly cornball. They incorporated genuine moral lessons about love, kindness, faith, and hope. They were both Christian and realistic, much to the inspiration and enjoyment of his legion of viewers.

Capra regarded *It's a Wonderful Life* (1947) as his ultimate triumph. "It was produced with no concern for the critics," he wrote. "I thought it was the greatest film I ever made," he added. "Better yet,"if we allow him a bit of self-congratulations, "I thought it was the greatest film anybody ever made. It wasn't made for the oh-so-bored critics or the oh-so-jaded literati. It was my kind of film for my kind of people". Nonetheless, this timeless Christmas classic earned him an Oscar nomination. He previously won the coveted Oscar for directing his 1934 romantic comedy, *It Happened One Night.*

It's a Wonderful Life could easily be re-titled as "Life Is a Wonderful Gift". Just as Christmas is about giving, starting with God the Father giving us His Son, so is life. Capra's classic now stands with Charles Dicken's *A Christmas Carol* as the most treasured Christmas stories we see each year at Christmas time. The former involves a man from Hell, Jacob Marley, who shows Ebenezer Scrooge the ruinous future he is preparing for himself and for others. The latter involves an angel from heaven, Clarence Odbody, who shows George Bailey what a wonderful life he has had. In both stories the order of time is changed so that the trajectory of the two lives can be seen from the perspective of eternity. Also central to the stories are the families of Bob Cratchit and George Bailey (played by Jimmy Stewart). Both stories reveal how each person can have a profound effect on the lives of others, especially on intimates, according to how he views the significance of his life.

Christmas is about eternity since it represents the eternal God coming into a world of time. It is the conjunction between the timeless and the temporal. It offers us, therefore, an occasion to reflect on our lives and consider where we are going. It beckons us to see our lives in a larger perspective and to think about the relationship between our birth and our destiny. Christ's birth is inseparable from his destiny. The light He brings into the world is one that illuminates all of human history.

This larger perspective, achieved at Christmas time in both of these timeless stories, is needed for the conversions of the two central characters: Ebenezer Scrooge and George Bailey. Given a frame of reference that transcends the moment, they come to realize the essential importance of love and generosity. They come to understand that life is a blessing, one that must be shared with others. Both the

Bailey and the Cratchit families are the immediate beneficiaries of this insight. They are the beneficiaries of what Christmas throughout the year represents.

This Christmas, we might reserve a moment to thank Frank Capra for his many cinematic gifts, especially, *It's A Wonderful* Life, and for his vision and his integrity.

The Significance of Language

Language exists for the purpose of communication. It unites people by allowing them to share a common experience of reality. The Word was made Flesh and dwelt among us.

God is the Word and the *Logos*. Dialogue means speaking across the *Logos*, or sharing in the meaning of that which is both real and rational. There can be no communion, community, or dialogue in the absence of meaning that is accessible and knowledgeable for all people. The Trinity is an eternal dialogue between the Father, Son, and Holy Spirit.

Concomitant with the eclipse of God, language no longer communicates something that is real, and therefore sharable by everyone. It has degenerated into an ideology that supports one group but is unintelligible to others. The importance of using words properly is powerfully stated in Matthew 12:36: "But I say unto you, that every idle word that men shall speak, they shall give account thereof in the Day of Judgment".

Below are brief analyses of 10 commonly used words that are used, not to communicate reality, but to promote an ideology. The first five words are used in such a restricted way as to block out other legitimate uses of the word. The next five words are used so broadly as to convey far more than what they are intended to mean and therefore mean nothing.

Discriminate: This word has been truncated so that it no longer means "to make reasonable distinctions"—this is a dog and not a cat; this is an adult and not a teenager—but to discriminate unjustly. Thus, a blind fencer in Canada feels that he is being discriminated against because he is not allowed to fence with competitors who are sighted. Anyone can make the charge that he is a victim of discrimination simply because he or she is called male or female, lean or heavy, tall or short. A reasonable distinction can be misunderstood as a stereotype and therefore a form of discrimination.

Impose: This word is used so broadly that it includes making a suggestion, ministering to another's needs, or stating a position. Thus, Notre Dame University students objected to a distinguished speaker for merely stating the values of Christian virtues. "He was trying to impose his values on us," they cried. "Imposing" is now a fearful word that represents, in the minds of many, taking away one's freedom.

Choose: This is the sacred word of pro-abortionists. What is egregiously omitted is any reference to what is chosen. But choice is not self-justifying since arson, murder, and rape can also be choices. As an intellectual faculty, the ability to choose is a gift from God. What we choose, however, may be evil. The faculty and the use of the faculty are two different enterprises.

Hate: Hate is contrary to love and is unacceptable. But hate is now disagreement with an ideology. A 17-year of high school student in Manitoba was suspended for objecting to wearing an LGBT poppy. She thought that honoring this group on the same level as that of the soldiers who fought and died for Canada was an outrage. What seemed more important, however, was how the LGBT group reacted to it. The student had committed a "hate crime".

Offend: Thou shall not offend seems to be an 11th commandment these days. People find the Lord's Prayer offensive, honoring the flag of one's country, red and green colored cookies at Christmas, and virtually anything that does not conform to their arbitrary ideology. No regard is given, however, to the people that the hyper-sensitive ideologues are truly offending. Offending God does not seem to be a matter of concern.

Diversity: Diversity is merely a word, not a philosophy. As such it is neutral. It is desirable or undesirable in relation to what it includes. If it is comprised of harmonious elements, then it can be good. On the other hand, if it consists of warring elements, then it is bad. The current use of "diversity" is ideological and excludes anyone who does not share that ideology. To praise the diversity of God's Creation is not considered an acceptable way of celebrating diversity.

Inclusivity: Christianity violates the narrow dogma of inclusivity by excluding both sin as well as the Devil. Inclusivity pertains only to those groups or individuals that profess an allegiance to what is truly an exclusive group. It makes no sense to support inclusivity if its membership includes contradictories, such as Jews and Nazis. Inclusivity is a buzz word for those who prefer not to think.

Rights: Genuine rights are relatively few and are usually associated with duties. The new notion of rights is synonymous with desires. At the extreme edge, militant ideologists believe they have the right to violate other people's rights. One group has the right to do pretty much anything it pleases while denying another groups its right to defend itself against unjust aggression. In documented instances, children have been accorded the "right" to choose their own sexual identity while their parents are not allowed the right in intervene. Rights were recognized not for the purpose of starting friction, but in an attempt to avoid them and establish justice.

Equality: We are equal as human beings and unequal in sundry ways. Heterosexual and homosexual marriages cannot be equal since they are fundamentally different. But an unborn child and one that is born are equally members of the human family. Yet equal rights for the pre-born and the post-born are not recognized. By the misuse of the word "equality," un-equals are seen as equals while equals are regarded as un-equals. Injustice is pandemic.

Dignity: Dignity has two legitimate meanings. The first applies to the seal that God has placed on the human soul by which it has an unalienable worth or dignity. The second meaning pertains to a manner in which one comports himself or a favorable condition. One can gain or lose dignity in the second sense of the term. However, one cannot lose the dignity that is an indelible characteristic of his being. Therefore, the popular notion of "death with dignity" is grossly misleading since it implies that without some form of mercy killing, one would forfeit his essential dignity.

The Kindness of Light

Light in Winter is the title of the second volume of Meriol Trevor's definitive biography of John Henry Newman. It may have been a source of considerable inspiration, if not grace, for Miss Trevor to have written the biography while living in one of the cottages at Littlemore, Newman's original retreat, where he prayed, fasted, and studied before being received into the Catholic Church in 1845.

Saint John Henry Newman's great work was to shed light in a darkened world. "Light," for one of the Church's more recently canonized saints, is both theological, helping to clarify the reality of God and the teachings of the Church, as well as philosophical illuminating the proper object of the intellect, which is Truth.

Newman's life spanned the 19th century, from 1801 to 1890. Bishop Clifford, who, as a student in Rome had served Newman's first Mass, preached at the Cardinal's funeral service. One sentence in the eulogy perfectly epitomized Newman's life: "God, in His tender mercy towards this land, chose him for a special work and endowed him with gifts especially fitting him for that work".

"Light" and "work" were intimately intertwined throughout Newman's career. In 1832, while in Castro Giovanni, Sicily, Newman had a severe attack of fever and nearly died. In fact, he was sufficiently convinced that he was going to die, he made final arrangements with his Italian servant. The illness kept him in bed for three weeks. Nonetheless, in a memorandum describing his sickness, which he wrote years later, he stated: "As I lay in bed the first day, many thoughts came over me . . . I felt and kept saying to myself, 'I have not sinned against the light' . . . God has still a work for me to do." Indeed, as it turned out, God had a great deal of work for Newman to do.

When Newman's condition had greatly improved, he left Sicily on a boat bound for Marseilles. But his ship was becalmed for an entire week between Corsica and Sardinia in the Straits of Bonifacio. It was on this occasion that Newman penned his most endearing poem, which begins as follows: "Lead Kindly light, amid the encircling gloom,/Lead Thou me on/The Night is dark, and I am far from home – Lead Thou me on".

The poem brings to mind several things: Newman's own loneliness, depressed spirit, and homesickness, as well as the gloom of the world, the darkness of man's intellect, and the eclipse of God. The enveloping multi-levelled darkness moved Newman to recognize, with great emotional force, both the necessity and the compelling significance of light. It was an experience that would remain with him for a lifetime.

Newman was utterly convinced that because he had not sinned against the light, God has an important work for him to perform. Pope Leo XIII, in his encyclical, *Aeterni Patris*, had denounced intellectual sins against the light, while urging his readers to dispel the darkness of error. Gerard Phelan, who supervised the French to English translation Jacques Maritain's classic *The Degrees of Knowledge*, stated that the cause of the malady afflicting the modern mind "is a suicidal decision of philosophers to disown completely the proper function of the intelligence and to place as the first condition of all knowledge an initial sin against the light".

Newman's canonization is a strong affirmation of the importance of philosophy and, one hopes, will encourage many to follow his example. At the close of his book, *On the Scope and Nature of University Education*, he had these parting words for his readers: "What I would urge upon every one, whatever may be his particular line of research, - what I would urge upon men of science in their thoughts of Theology, -- what I would venture to recommend to theologians, when their attention is drawn to the subject of scientific investigations, -- is a great and firm belief in the sovereignty of Truth."

The "sovereignty of Truth" is an elegant phrase. It stands along with *Cor ad cor loquitur* ("Heart speaking to Heart", the motto which Newman took adopted when he was made Cardinal) as capturing in a minimum of words, the essence of Newman's mind and heart.

The Idea of a University is Newman's most popular work. For Newman, the cultivation of a gentleman is not the same thing as the development of a Christian. In the absence of theology, education is radically incomplete. The mere gentleman, important as he is in his own right, is ill-suited to deal with the temptations of the world. Newman is considered to be, in addition to his many other gifts, a literary genius. We find numerous examples of literary eloquence throughout the pages of *The Idea of a University*. In pointing out the difficulty in establishing honest communication with certain people, he has this to say: "Quarry the granite rock with razors, or moor the vessel with a thread of silk; then you may hope with such keen and delicate instruments as human knowledge and human reason to contend against those giants, the passion and the pride of man." By no means, was Newman as cynic. But he was not naïve to the difficulties in communicating with certain individuals. Martin Buber has remarked that the inability to communicate "is the most acute symptom of the pathology of our time".

Saint John Henry Newman was canonized on October 13, 2019 before an estimated 20,000 pilgrims. He is the first Briton to be so honored in 43 years. On the occasion, Prince Charles accurately described him as a "fearless defender of the truth". Saint Newman is most assuredly a saint for out troubled times. He is a beacon of light for our darkening winter.

The Naturalness of Thanks

"The proud man counts his newspaper clippings," Bishop Sheen once remarked, "the humble man his blessings". Counting one's blessings is an expression of gratitude. The grateful person understands that the giver is more important than the gift, and therefore should be honored. Adam and Eve were given much, but they were lacking in the one thing they could give back: gratitude.

One may recall the lyrics to the Irving Berlin song from the 1954 movie, *White Christmas*: "When I'm worried and I can't sleep, I count my blessings instead of sheep". Gratitude can confer benefits on the grateful recipient, namely, peace of heart. Like mercy, as Shakespeare states in *The Merchant of Venice,* gratitude is twice blessed.

We can become so enamored with a gift that we forget what we owe to the giver. Saying thanks is a small price for a gift. It is the best bargain that we will ever have. And yet, for reasons that are both perplexing and mysterious, people often find it either difficult or unnecessary to express gratitude.

Luke (17:12-19) recounts the story of the ten lepers whom Jesus cured. What remains most striking about this episode is not the miraculous cure (we expect that of the son of God), but why only one of the ten returned to offer thanks. Christ asks, "Were not all made clean?   The other nine, where are they?" We sense disappointment in his words. And we are surprised, if not astonished at the nine lepers who did not see fit to offer thanks. One would think that being suddenly and completely cured of this dreadful affliction would inspire thanks. The nine lepers, however, needed to be cured on a spiritual level. But thanks is something that springs from the heart. We cannot force another to give thanks. The metaphysical poet, George Herbert, refers to this troubling reluctance on the part of human beings to offer thanks when he writes: "Thou hast given so much to me. Give me one thing more, a grateful heart".

"How sharper than a serpent's tongue," wrote Shakespeare, "to have a thankless child" (*King Lear,* I.4, 310-11). We wonder about how Christ was offended by the ungrateful lepers, and how God was offended by the inappreciation for his gifts shown by Adam and Eve. The virtue of gratitude, as Bishop Sheen has indicated, is intimately connected with humility. We owe each other more than we can count. We are highly dependent beings, a fact that should humble us. We need gifts, beginning with the gift of life. Saying "thank you" is a recognition that we cannot make a decent life for ourselves all by ourselves. Our debt of gratitude toward others is inexhaustible. The words of Albert Schweitzer come to mind: "At times our own light goes out and is rekindled by a spark from another person. Each of us has cause to think with deep gratitude of those who have lighted the flame within us". A simple "thank you" can spur us on. It is akin to the baton that relay runners pass on to each other on their way to victory.

According to an ancient Jewish legend, after God completed creation, he asked the angels what they thought of it. One of them replied that the world is so vast and perfect that there was nothing wanting except an expression of gratitude. Yet, so many are so reluctant to complete the work of creation by uttering a simple thank you. It is somewhat of a theological mystery as to why gratitude is not as common as it should be. Too many people spend more time grumbling about their problems than being grateful about what they have.

Gratitude is the choice to remain friends with God. It is doing our part, small as it is, to applaud what He has given us. It is a modest echo to a grand performance. Abraham Lincoln knew something about human nature when he commented that "we are prone to forget the source from which they [our blessings] come". Therefore, on October 3, 1863 he issued a Proclamation establishing the last Thursday of November "as a day of Thanksgiving and Praise to our Father who dwelleth in the Heavens".

The Civil War was still raging at that time. The Proclamation calls for thanksgiving, but it also begs God for healing: "[We] fervently implore the interposition of the Almighty Hand to heal the wounds of the nation and to restore it as soon as possible as may be consistent with the divine purposes to the full enjoyment of peace, harmony, tranquility and Union". While we offer thanks, in 2019, we should also ask for forgiveness to atone for all the moments in the past when we failed to give thanks.

The pilgrims are credited with inaugurating the tradition of Thanksgiving in America. In 1777, a year after the Declaration of Independence, the Continental Congress declared a day of thanksgiving to celebrate a Revolutionary War victory over the British at Saratoga. George Washington declared a day of thanksgiving and prayer in 1789, in part, to honor the new United States constitution. But it took the trauma of the Civil War to make Thanksgiving a formal, annual holiday. Giving thanks during a time of turmoil may be gratitude's sincerest form of expression. Moreover, it continues the line of development that begins with humility, passes through gratitude, and culminates in hope.

The true spirit of Christmas is often sidetracked due to shopping for presents. The true meaning of Thanksgiving is often obscured by football. Despite the formality of these holidays, we must continue to make the effort to appreciate them for what they are worth. We must remember to be thankful for all our blessings at every Thanksgiving.

The Warmth of the Heart

"Have a heart" is a popular idiom: "I am sorry for what I said, please have a heart and forgive me." It does, however, raise an interesting question: "Is it possible for a person not to possess this vital organ"? Can a person truly be heartless, if only for a moment? The heart is at the very core of our personality. This statement may appear redundant since the word "core" is derived from the Latin *cor*, which refers to the heart. At any rate, the heart is an essential and indelible part of us. We cannot rid ourselves entirely of our heart.

What we mean when we implore a person to "have a heart" is to get his heart functioning in the proper way. The heart should be a source of virtue and nothing less. When our heart is not expressing itself virtuously, it may create the impression that a person is "heartless". The heart is versatile and spacious, capable of many things, some good, some not so good. The heart is multilayered and polyvalent. The Pseudo-Macarius has expressed the matter admirably: "The heart itself is but a small vessel, yet dragons live there, and there are many lions; there are poisonous beasts and all the treasures of evil. But there too is God, the angels, the life and the kingdom, the light and the apostles, the heavenly cities and the treasures of grace— all things are there." We would do well to take his message to heart.

Three virtues of the heart, in particular, that should be cheerfully employed during the Christmas Season are warm-heartedness, lightheartedness, and kind-heartedness. Charles Dickens' immortal classic, *A Christmas Carol*, is about the transformation of Ebenezer Scrooge's heart from something icy cold to something vibrant and bursting with joy.

Early in the tale, Dickens describes Scrooge as an ice-cold character whose heart is bereft of any warmth: "The cold within him froze his old features, nipped his pointed nose, shriveled his cheek, stiffened his gait, made his eyes red, his thin lips blue, and spoke out shrewdly in his grating voice. A frosty rime was on his head, and on his eyebrow, and on his wiry chin. He carried his own low temperature always within him; he iced his office in the dog days; and didn't thaw it one degree at Christmas." A novelist can make his character utterly unattractive simply by reducing the temperature of his heart.

Dante's Ninth Circle of Hell is a frozen lake in which Satan is eternally trapped. Scrooge was heading in that direction until his heart underwent a radical conversion. A heart of ice is a heart of vice. We read in Luke 24:32 about the two companions who walked with Jesus on the road to Emmaus. "Did not our hearts burn within us while he talked to us on the road, while he opened to us the scriptures?" The warmth of Jesus' heart touched them just as the warmth of a fireplace warms those who are close to it. Warm-heartedness is infectious. It communicates itself to others without effort. The virtue of warm-heartedness, like modesty, is recognized apart from its being expressed in a particular action. If there must be global warming let it arise from the collectivity of happy hearts.

Through the intercession of the spirits of the past, present, and future, Scrooge's heart began functioning at full throttle. The virtues of warm-heartedness, lightheartedness, and kind-heartedness were activated simultaneously, which made Scrooge's whole being go into a spin. "I don't know what to do!" cried Scrooge, laughing and crying in the same breath; . . . "I am as light as a feather, I am as happy as an angel, I am as merry as a schoolboy. I am as giddy as a drunken man. A merry Christmas to everybody! A happy New Year to all the world. Hallo here! Whoop! Hallo!" The "bah, humbug" of the cynic had faded into the distant past. He now went about wishing everyone in sight a Merry Christmas laughing all the way. As Dickens states, "His own heart laughed; and that was quite enough for him." Scrooge had unburdened himself from the weight of monetary concerns which freed him to be light-hearted. G. K. Chesterton famously stated that angels can fly because they take themselves lightly.

Warm-heartedness and lightheartedness had made it easy for him to be kindhearted. Scrooge purchased the prize turkey, twice the size of Tiny Tim, and dispatched it anonymously to the Cratchit family. His heart was bursting with virtue so much so that he promised to give his longsuffering employee a raise and committed himself to assisting his struggling family. Tiny Tim would receive his life-saving operation. "Shall not my heart's warming," wrote Robert Browning, "not nurse thee into strength?"

The nineteenth century Nova Scotian humorist, Thomas C. Haliburton once remarked that "God has made sunny spots in the heart; why should we exclude the light from them." *Proverbs* 17; 22 reminds us that "A cheerful heart is good medicine." The three spirits who visited Ebenezer Scrooge had awakened his "sunny spots" and provided him with strong medicine. And in so doing, brought him back to life. Virtue is the vitality of the heart.

Wishing people a "Merry Christmas" is a very lighthearted thing to do. Gifts are expressions of kindheartedness. Warm-heartedness is the glow that radiates from all who observe the joy that Christmas brings. Christmas is a time when these virtues of the heart should be fully on display. They resonate the joy of the first Christmas and the singing of angels.

Tiny Tim has the last word in Dickens' classic, "God bless Us Every One," affirming Dickens' own words: "For it is good to be children sometimes, and never better than at Christmas, when its mighty Founder was a child Himself."

The Realism of Philosophy

Culture changes. We bid goodbye to somethings and welcome others. We do not miss the hula hoop or Nehru jackets, but we cannot do without email and compact discs. Most unfortunately, however, in the kaleidoscope of change, somethings that are indispensable are squeezed out. I am speaking here of the untimely dismissal of philosophy as the love of wisdom. Is philosophy really dead? Prof. Lewis Samuel Feuer, a sociologist and Professor Emeritus of the University of Virginia has put it bluntly, "American philosophy is dead". His pronouncement was reported in *The New York Times*, though not in the obituary column.

The situation is "peculiar and even strange," observed the distinguished philosopher Josef Pieper in *The Future of Thomism* (1992). Scepticism, relativism, cynicism, and deconstruction have pushed true philosophy into virtual oblivion.The problem that philosophy now faces is not this or that issue that is germane to the philosophical enterprise, but, as Pieper laments, "Why philosophy at all?"

What has happened in contemporary culture that is inimical to philosophy? We might take a cursory look at three factors: democracy, progress, and affluence. These factors are all good in themselves, but when they are not properly understood, they become enemies of philosophy.

Democracy stresses the notion of equality. This is fine as long as it does not demean distinctiveness. Everyone has an equal right to vote, but not everyone is equally wise. When equality suppresses distinctiveness, the claim is made that no one is more right or wrong than anyone else. Philosophy students, therefore, are not less wise than their teachers. Children are not less wise than their parents. Plato and Aquinas are of merely historic interest. They have nothing to teach us. One man's philosophy is as good as the thought of any other man. Hugh Hefner has nothing to learn from Aristotle.

Democracy, in the proper sense, demands education. In Ray Bradbury's novella, Fahrenheit 451°, all books must be burned since, after reading a book, a person will think he is no longer equal to his neighbor. Equality, however, relates more to opportunity than it does to achievement. In a democracy, not everyone will take full advantage of his opportunity. The central irony of democracy is that while it welcomes equality of opportunity, it also praises inequality of achievement. Philosophy as love of wisdom is one of the great achievements of democracy properly understood.

Progress is only too apparent. In science and its applied fields, ranging from medicine to computers, the fact that there is progress is unarguable. But it is not at all apparent that there has been progress in morality. General Omar N. Bradley said it well when he made the comment that "Ours is a world of nuclear giants and ethical infants. We know more about war than we know about peace, more about killing than about living. We have grasped the mystery of the atom and rejected the Sermon on the Mount."

Progress is often confused with change. With change there is also novelty. And novelty passes for progress. Scripture tells us that there is nothing new under the sun. The nature of the human being, his divine origin, his destiny and moral responsibilities persist. They are constants. The great danger of novelty is to erase the best of tradition, whatever wisdom has been passed down from generation to generation concerning the human drama. Novelty is always new, seldom important, and never progressive in the truest sense of the word.

Philosophy that seeks an understanding of the nature of the human person and his essential responsibilities in life has no need of novelty. When novelty replaces philosophy it replaces wisdom along with it. Thus, philosophy is commonly derogated as atavistic, belonging to the Middle Ages, and the attempt to impose one's private values on another. Novelty, however, is doomed to be replaced by an ensuing wave of novelty. Philosophy is timeless, novelty belongs to today but not to tomorrow.

Affluence relates to material or financial prosperity. In itself, it is something to be cherished. However, affluence brings into play the powerful temptation to make wealth the ultimate object of one's life. When this occurs, wisdom loses its primacy. Love of money, the root of all evil as the Bible notes, breeds a disdain for wisdom. The rich man has considerable problems working his way through the eye of a needle in order to gain entrance into heaven.

The catch phrase, "the one who dies with the most money wins," reveals the emptiness of wealth as a life goal. Life is not a sport. It is not about an accumulation of material goods, but a personal expression of love and obedience to the Will of God. One cannot carry his financial assets into the Promised Land.

Democracy, progress, and affluence are limited goods. Each one of them needs to be complemented by wisdom. Without wisdom, they become caricatures of themselves, no longer serving human beings but becoming their enemies. In the contemporary world, when philosophy attempts to make its entrance it is rebuffed as a kind of disease. One example should be sufficient. The philosophical judgment that certain sexual acts between the same sexes are unnatural, although solidly rooted in both Scripture as well as in science, is routinely dismissed as "homophobic". Rational discussion, therefore, is precluded. The person who purports to be a philosopher, a lover of wisdom, is maligned as someone who is operating from a disease.

In this world where democracy, progress, and affluence are given far more significance that they deserve, is there any room left for philosophy? Even though philosophy is not a characteristic at the present moment of the surrounding culture, it will continue to be a prized possession for certain individuals. Nevertheless, they should know what they are battling against. One must be courageous before he becomes wise. Philosopher Jacques Maritain has a word of hope when he comments that despite the cultural stifling of the intellect, it 'cannot be affected in its essential constitution". In other words, the sun continues to exist even when clouds cover the sky.

The Splendor of Knowledge

The word "cosmos" was coined by Pythagoras and referred to a universe that is unified, ordered, good, and beautiful. The latter adjective endures among cosmetologists whose work with cosmetics are aimed at restoring beauty to the face. According to Hesiod, chaos was the first thing that came to be. Many religious groups in ancient Greece believed that chaos was nothingness, but not entirely inert. It was a matrix of unintelligible entities from which things took shape and became distinct, ultimately forming the cosmos. Given the intimacy between cosmos and chaos, it was inevitable that people would fear that the cosmos would eventually return to that vast amorphous soup known as chaos.

These terms were not created out of thin air. They were based on philosophical responses to the visible world. On the one hand, the order of the universe was apparent. The planets moved in regular patterns, day and night alternated predictably, the seasons followed in a consistent manner, and people organized their lives in accordance with the sunrise and the sunset. On the other hand, there was turmoil: volcanic eruptions, hurricanes, typhoons, and tornados. On the human level: war, famines, pestilence, and plagues of a variety of kinds. Which term, then, cosmos or chaos, accurately captures the nature of the universe?

This distinction has particular relevance for how human beings should live. For, if chaos is the proper name of the universe, then vice is the appropriate comportment for human beings. But if the universe is a cosmos, then human beings should order their lives through virtue. The fact that the Greeks distinguished between the microcosm man and the macrocosm world indicated that people could live in harmony with the universe. Man is merely a microcosm, but one through which he can understand the order of the macrocosm world.

The modern world has become skeptical about the meaning of life. There seems to be an unhealable severance between the microcosm man and the macrocosm world. Man no longer "knows", he just "thinks". We think a great deal, although we seldom come to a conclusion. The consequence of this inconclusive thinking is the politically correct view that all opinions are equal. Truth disappears and conjecture reigns.

It is significant, as Anton Pegis, an expert in medieval philosophy, has pointed out, that St. Thomas Aquinas did not have in his vocabulary a word corresponding to the term "thinker". Such a term cannot be translated into Latin. For Aquinas, man is a "knower", not a "thinker". Obviously, man thinks, but as a "mere thinker" he does not achieve knowledge. From the viewpoint of the Angelic Doctor, the decline of medieval philosophy was really a transition from man as a "knower" to man as a "thinker". According to Pegis, a "thinker" in this sense is a "disexistentialized knower".

"I think therefore I am", Descartes' deathless phrase, locks the self in a prison, shut off from anything beyond itself. We are descendants of Descartes whether we realize it or not.

Albert Einstein once said that the most incomprehensible thing for him was that the universe is comprehensible. In other words, how was the mind of man attuned to the order of the universe so that man could know something about the universe? The answer to this question, which vexes scientists, is best explained theologically. God created man a knower and one who would build his love on what he knew. Therefore, God created man to be an integral part of the universe, knowingly connected with its laws.

The frequency emitted by a radio station is attuned to the radio (or receiving set). Of course, this connection does not happen by chance. It was designed. So, too, the connection between the knower and what is known must also be ordered. We take this for granted when listening to the radio, but neglect two more extraordinary attunements, between our ear and what it senses, and our mind which interprets the meaning of what we hear. We are knowers who live in a cosmos, not mere thinkers who dwell in chaos.

The notion of chaos has a firm place in the world of fantasy. Video games, movies, recordings, novels, comic books, and radio and TV programs make steady and effective use of it. Chaos is attractive and intriguing because it is daring, rebellious, exciting, and adventurous. In the world of fantasy, anything that is well-ordered, by contrast, seems frightfully boring.

In the field of mathematics, the phrase "chaos theory" may be misleading. It is not the case that mathematics is chaotic in itself, but it is the mathematician's admission that there are vast areas of reality that cannot the correlated with mathematics. Indeterminacy and unpredictability are confessions of human ignorance, not the presence of disorder in the universe.

Scripture informs us that God created the world out of nothing. He did not bring the cosmos out from chaos. In creating out of nothing, he manifested his infinite power, but also brought into being a cosmos that was entirely separate from any notion of chaos. There are times in our lives when we have a perception of this truth, that God's creation is His work and His work alone.

The Gift of Nature

I was finishing my morning coffee and nothing in particular was occupying my mind. A Black-capped Chickadee suddenly appeared before my eyes, crawling along the sides of our front-yard maple tree. It was busy, no doubt looking for food. At that moment it seemed to be operating with more purpose than I was. This tiny little oviparous vertebrate has a special knack for finding bird feeders. Consequently, it has become a rather popular bird. It also has the reputation of being "cute". Its black cap and bib, white cheeks, gray back and whitish underside make it distinctive and easy to recognize. This feathered creature was not only my morning's entertainment, but a philosophical inspiration.

I am always impressed by the fact than animals, so magnificently designed to do what they are supposed to do, just go about their business and never stop to reflect on how marvellously created they are. When the chickadee arrives in the Fall, its brain neurons die and along with them, old information. New neurons are formed so that new information can guide it through changes in the environment and their social flocks. Despite the small size of its brain, the Chickadee calls are complex and communicate information on the identity and recognition of other flocks as well as sending out alarms. The more "dee" notes it calls out indicate a higher level of threat. All this, of course, astonishes me, especially in the light of the fact that so many intelligent people deny that there is such a thing as Intelligent Design.

My early morning rapture took me back to my science days when I studied zoology. My text was Tracy I. Storer's *General Zoology*. The author states, with no suggestion of amazement, that "In some moths the odor of a female may attract a male for a mile or more". Could it have happened by sheer chance that the male moth can distinguish the specific odor of the female among the innumerable smells that fill the atmosphere? It is like having a radio that is tuned to a specific frequency that is the only one needed to locate its mate. Is this synchrony purely a matter of chance? Imagine a telephone number imprinted on a child's hand which corresponds to the telephone number of the person he is destined to marry? Would this be chance or design?

Ruminating further into the marvels of the animal kingdom, I came across the following: "The female butterfly carries a store of perfume weighing only 1/10,000 of a milligram, and she squirts minute fraction of it into the air. These scent molecules can be detected by a male seven miles away". St. Thomas Aquinas would have taken this fact in stride. In his *Summa Theologica* he writes, "We see that things which lack knowledge, such as natural bodies, act for an end, and this is evident from their acting always, or nearly always, in the same ways, so as to obtain their end, not fortuitously, but designedly." And he is right: spiders spin webs, beavers build dams, ants form anthills, and bees make honey.

Let us consider the "coincidences" that are involved that lead to the ultimate mating of our butterfly: 1) that a specific perfume is stored in the body of the female butterfly; 2) that she has an organ that allows her to release the perfume into the air; 3) the instinct on the part of the butterfly to know when to release the perfume; 4) the structure of the perfume molecules to remain in the air while travelling over a radius of seven miles; 5) the ability of the male butterfly to detect the perfume; 6) the fact that the male finds the perfume alluring; 7) the ability of the male to track down the origin of the perfume; 8) that the female will accept the male when he arrives; 9) the mating and all the complexity involved therein; 10) the progeny that are subsequently produced.

All these factors must be simultaneously present so that the purpose of reproduction is achieved. For example, if the male butterfly does not find the perfume alluring, the chain is broken and reproduction cannot take place. If the butterflies are not equipped with the proper and complementary organs, the chain is likewise broken. Charles Darwin contended that changes in species happen one at a time. He has no provision for a multitude of factors becoming co-present at the same time. In his *Origin of the Species*, he makes the following statement: "If it could be demonstrated that any complex organ existed which could not possibly be formed by numerous, successive, slight modifications, my theory would absolutely break down."

Darwin was an indefatigable student of nature. Despite his extensive knowledge, however, his evolutionary theory does not hold. It was a theory, not something that anyone could observe. He penned his classic in 1859 at a time when molecular biology had yet to be discovered. He was, therefore, laboring under a severe handicap. He was trying to get the most out of natural selection and the survival of the fittest, but his contention, as he feared, did not allow for the simultaneous existence of a multiplicity of factors that could not have evolved one step at a time. The Chickadee, the moth, and the butterfly remained an insolvable puzzle for him.

My tiny visitor has fled but has awakened me. For this I am grateful, though he will never be able to appreciate that fact. So, I express my gratitude to God for having created such a splendid creature while recalling the words of Gerard Manley Hopkins: "Glory be to God for dappled things . . . He fathers-forth whose beauty is past change: Praise him".

On one of his expeditions to the South Pole, Admiral Richard E. Byrd recorded an experience he had while situated near the Bay of Whales. It was twilight, that time of day when it seems that chaos is absorbing the cosmos into itself. At this moment, Admiral Byrd seemed to be in tune with the music of the spheres. "It was enough to catch the rhythm, momentarily, to be myself a part of it," he wrote. "In that instant I could feel no doubt of man's oneness with the universe . . . It was a feeling that transcended reason that went to the heart of man's despair and found it groundless. The universe was a cosmos, not a chaos".

It is the cosmos that is real. The ancient Greeks could not fathom a God who created from nothing, and so they invented chaos. At the same time, we should remember that sin is a choice for chaos, which is not only a choice for disorder, but a choice for nothingness.

The Fulfillment of Education

The philosophy teacher provides a service. He is not in the least interested in imposing particular ideas on his students. He is well aware that it is not possible, literally, to impose an abstract idea on anyone. In his presentation, he puts a series of ideas on display. Students find some of these ideas attractive and others unattractive. In this regard, the philosophy teacher is like a grocer in a grocery store who displays a variety of foods. His customers find some of the foods on display, but not all, to be attractive. Philosophy students are selective consumers of ideas; grocery store shoppers are selective consumers of food products.

Students in a philosophy classroom, however, often act very differently from the consumers in a grocery store. A student, when presented with an idea he does not like may react with outrage, fearing that that idea might harm him. Ideas of God, abortion, euthanasia, homosexuality, for example, may provoke outrage. The consumer in a grocery store never takes what he does not like personally. He calmly passes by the kumquats, caviar, and chocolate covered ants. What he does not like does not bother him. He is in control, purchasing only what he wants with undisturbed tranquility.

A philosophy teacher can be suspended or lose his job for displaying particular ideas on hot-button topics. The ultra-sensitive student insists that his teacher present only ideas that he finds agreeable. Consumers do not demand that the grocer provide only food products that suit their taste.

The philosophy teacher may envy the grocer, wishing that his students would view the ideas he offers in the classroom with the same emotional calm that consumers have when viewing the various products displayed at the grocery store. His envy would be understandable, though unacceptable. Comparisons between the philosopher and the grocer are legitimate, but very thin.

The philosopher and the grocer do indeed provide a service. They offer something that is beneficial. Their interest is not primarily for themselves. The grocer provides what his customers want; the philosophy teacher provides what his students need. It is one of the essential paradoxes of the human being not to want what he truly needs.

A student could count himself fortunate if he had Martin Buber, author of the classic, *I and Thou*, for a teacher. In an article entitled, *The Education of Character*, Buber recounts some of the difficulties he encountered as a teacher. When he tried to explain that envy is despicable, he is opposed by those who are poorer than their comrades. When he attempted to explain that it is wicked to bully the weak, he sees a half-disguised smile cross the lips of the strong. He feels the same frustration when he ventures to teach that lying destroys life. "But as soon as my students notice that I want to educate their characters I am resisted," he writes. And so, as Buber avers, "The test of the educator lies in conflict with his pupil".

The grocer operates under the maxim that the customer is always right. The philosopher knows that his pupils are often wrong. Conflict arises when the student commits himself to conforming to his culture or when he finds it too difficult to change. Therefore, he finds his own reasons to reject the eternal ideas of truth, beauty, goodness, and justice.

Eating is a common denominator for what is edible and what is understandable. We speak of food for the mind and how certain ideas are difficult to digest. Francis Bacon famously stated that "Some books are to be tasted, others to be swallowed, and some to be chewed and digested". Both food and ideas enter the person. However, the effect on the person can be different in a most important way.

Philosophy is in the business of love, in accord with its brief definition as "love of wisdom". Therefore, it is transformative. What we eat becomes us. Knowing about the eternal verities transforms us into something higher. This is why Saint Thomas Aquinas states that it is better to love God than to know a lion. Love changes us into that which we love. Knowledge, as well as eating, resides in us. C. S. Lewis, not well known for his poetry, has expressed the matter with irresistible clarity in his poem, "On a Theme from Nicolas of Cusa":

> *But when the soul partakes of good*
> *Or truth, which are her savoury food,*
> *By some far subtler chemistry*
> *It is not they that change, but she,*
> *Who feels them enter with the state*
> *Of conquerors her opened gate,*
> *Or, mirror-like, digests their ray*
> *By turning luminous as they.*

The philosophy teacher loves his students and therefore wants them to become more fully themselves through their integration of truth and goodness. In this way they become more God-like. The student, by contrast, may resist this kind of change since it requires giving up something and reaching for something new. The classroom and the grocery store, consequently, are radically different arenas. Their aims, however much they have in common, are ultimately distinctive. If the philosophy teacher has no higher aim than to supply his students with a variety of ideas, in the manner of a grocery store, then he has lost sight of the nobility of his profession. Difficulty should not be daunting; opposition should not be discouraging. The sustained effort will prove to be worthwhile. As Buber remarks, "The educator who helps to bring man back to his own unity will help to put him again face to face with God."

The Meaning of Memory

"Those who cannot remember the past are condemned to repeat it." This oft quoted phrase is attributed to the philosopher George Santayana. It was probably coined, however, by Edmund Burke when he said, "Those who don't know history are doomed to repeat it." A more trenchant version of the phrase should read: "Those who do not learn from the past are condemned to repeat its mistakes."

It appears that all the mistakes we now make are repetitions of earlier mistakes. If we could learn from the past, if that is possible, we would live in a mistake-free world. Such a utopian dream is not likely to occur. Nonetheless, in attempting to expose a contemporary mistake, we can allude to the consequences of that same mistake when it went unrectified in the past. This could be a sobering experience.

It was January 21, 1861 when a most dramatic event took place on the floor of the United States Senate. Jefferson Davis, who had graduated from West Point Military Academy, rose to the floor in his place and began speaking in a low tone of voice: "I rise, Mr. President, for the purpose of announcing to the Senate that the State of Mississippi, by a solemn ordinance of her people, in convention assembled, has declared her separation from the United States." He then paused, being overcome by emotion, re-gathered himself and proceeded, with increasing forcefulness. He reminded his colleagues of his long-held belief in state sovereignty and reiterated his firm rejection of the phrase, stated in the Declaration of Independence, that "all men are created equal," applied to blacks as well as whites.

Before concluding his remarks, he offered his "apology for any pain which, in the heat of discussion, I have inflicted." He expressed his hope for peaceful relations between the North and South. He did not believe that the slavery issue was divisive on a national level. He had his views; other had theirs. He believed there was a middle ground that could be achieved through compromise. America was, nonetheless, on the eve of the Great Civil War.

Republicans, for the most part, were not in agreement with Davis. One Southern Democrat, Andrew Johnson of Tennessee, who later became America's 17th President, was openly hostile. A few weeks after the Mississippi senator's farewell to the nation speech, Johnson had this to say: "I cannot understand how he [Jefferson Davis] can be willing to hail another banner . . . It seems to me that if I could not unsheath my sword in vindication of the flag of my country . . . I would return the sword to its scabbard. I would never sheathe it in the bosom of my mother! Never! Never!"

What great moral lessons did America learn from the Civil War? Did it learn that "all men are created equal"? She may have learned that black men and white men were equal, but only after they were born. The unborn remained unequal, devoid of the right to life, and not included the generic phrase, "All men are created equal".

John C. Calhoun of South Carolina, statesman for the Democratic Party, argued passionately for "diversity". What he meant by that word, however, was the diversity of slavery along with non-slavery. He called for equal rights in all the Federal territories and a cessation of all anti-slavery agitation in the North. What he meant by "rights," however, was the "right" to impose slavery. Stephen Douglas wanted people to be "free to do as they please, to have slavery or not, as they choose." His notion of "freedom," however, included the "freedom" to enslave. Compromise, very much like "compassion" today, was accorded a special reverence. But there can be no compromise between slavery and non-slavery just as there can be no compromise between being aborted and not being aborted.

The language that promoted slavery in the 19th century and led to the Civil War is strikingly similar to the language that now promotes abortion and leads to the terrible divisiveness that currently exists. How far this divisiveness will go is difficult to say, but its intensity seems to be increasing on a daily basis. The Governor of New York has declared that there is no room in his state for people who are defenders of uterine life.

Words such as freedom, diversity, right, compassion, compromise, and liberty have many shades of meaning and application. In one era they can all be recruited to support slavery; at another time they can be enlisted to rationalize abortion. The same words that can inspire us and set us on the right path can also betray us. They can educate; they can seduce. The devil knows well how to utilize the English language. The art of using words wisely is not something we have learned from history. We may have learned something about the evil of slavery, but as a nation we have yet to learn about the evil of abortion.

Abraham Lincoln, in 1864, remarked that "The world has never had a good definition of liberty, and the American people, just now, are in need of one. We all declare for liberty, but in using the same word we do not all mean the same thing." He went on to point out that liberty to one person could mean selfishness, the liberty to do as he pleases. To others it could mean liberty for a group. He regarded these two meaning as incompatible with each other. Liberty for the sheep is to be saved from the wolf, whereas liberty for the wolf is to ravage the sheep. As Lincoln explained, the word "liberty" can be used to promote "tyranny". "And precisely the same difference prevails today among us human creatures," stated America's 16th president, "even in the North, and all professing to love liberty".

And even today, words continue to mislead. We fail to learn from the mistakes of the past because we are limited, finite creatures. But we also fail because we do not know how to speak to each other, that is, by respecting words and using them honestly, consistently, properly, and wisely.

The Beauty of Harmony

The foregoing article chronicles a triumph of justice, and in so doing, establishes a basis for hope. It also makes clear that particular United States Supreme Court decisions do not always have the last word on moral issues. What may be called "Supreme" is not necessarily final.

On February 12, 2009, Keith Plessy and Phoebe Ferguson, descendants of both sides of the infamous 1896 *Plessy v. Ferguson* U.S. Supreme Court decision, announced the establishment of the Plessy Ferguson Foundation for Education and Reconciliation. The aim of the Foundation is to teach the history of the 1896 case and its effects on the American people. "It is no longer Plessy v. Ferguson," said Keith Plessy in a radio interview. "It is Plessy and Ferguson". That is the Omega of a long and arduous journey that established civil rights for black Americans.

The Alpha of the story began in 1890 when the state of Louisiana adopted a law providing for "equal but separate accommodations for the white and colored races" on its railroads. The word "separate" stood for what it meant. "Equal" was a euphemism for "unequal". This inequality was amply exemplified when States consistently underfunded black schools and provided them with substandard buildings, textbooks, and supplies. Inequality prevailed in restaurants, washrooms, hotels, and in other public facilities. Segregation and "inequality" would prove to be a most incandescent mixture.

Homer Plessy tested the legitimacy of the Louisiana law by sitting in the "white" section of a train and refusing to leave when told to do so. He was fined $25 and his case was subsequently heard by Judge John H. Ferguson of the Criminal Court of New Orleans. Ferguson saw fit to uphold the law. But the case was far from closed. Ultimately, the Louisiana law was challenged in the United States Supreme Court in 1986 on the grounds that it violated both the 13th and 14th amendments of the Constitution. What seemed to be a strong case, however, failed to win the verdict of the Supreme Court judges. By a vote of 7-1 the Court upheld the Louisiana law. In so doing, it affirmed and maintained the notion that blacks were "separate but equal".

The single dissenter in the case, was Judge John Marshall Harlan, who understood that maintaining segregation is irreconcilable with true equality. His dissenting voice was passionate and eminently reasonable. "The white race deems itself to be dominant," he wrote, but the Constitution recognizes "no superior, dominant ruling class of citizens." "Our Constitution is colorblind," he went on to state, "In respect of civil rights all citizens are equal before the law." He summarized the equality of the races, independent of social status, in a precise and eloquent phrase: "The humblest is the peer of the most powerful".

Justice Harlan, known to posterity as the Great Dissenter, wrote a dissent that is worth reading in its entirety. One passage merits reiteration: "The destinies of the two races, in this country, are indissolubly linked together, and the interests of both require that the common government of all shall not permit the seeds of race hate to be planted under the sanction of law. What can more certainly arouse race hate, what more certainly create and perpetuate a feeling of distrust between these races, than state enactments which, in fact, proceed on the ground that colored citizens are so inferior and degraded that they cannot be allowed to sit in public coaches occupied by white citizens? That, as all will admit, is the real meaning of such legislation as was enacted in Louisiana."

The "Great Dissenter" also played the role of the "Astute Predictor". "In my opinion," he declared, "the judgment this day rendered will, in time prove to be quite as pernicious as the decision made by this tribunal in the Dred Scott Case". Fifty-eight years later, in *Brown v. Board of Education* (1954), the U.S. Supreme Court ruled that segregation in public education was unconstitutional. Ten years after that, the Civil Rights Act of 1964 prohibited all legal segregation. One may hope that the *Roe v. Wade* ruling of 1973 will, one day, also be overturned. The road to justice may be long and hard.

An historical marker was unveiled on February 12, 2009, as mentioned above, near the location where Homer Plessy had boarded his train. The marker reminds us that we should not forget the lessons of history. History is a teacher. Its lessons can be either inspiring or heartbreaking. If we do learn from history, we should imitate the best and avoid the worst.

Nonetheless, people are not always good students in the classroom of history. What was learned from the horrors of World War I that could have prevented World War II? How much about racial equality was learned from the time of the Dred Scott decision to *Plessy v. Ferguson*? Why does the spectre of Communism continue to raise its head? History is a teacher but not the most reliable one. In this regard, religion is its master.

Learning from history is learning from its mistakes. Ideally, one would like to avoid the mistakes. The philosopher George Santayana famously stated that if we do not learn from history, we are condemned to repeat its mistakes. On the other hand, Clarence Darrow maintains that "History repeats itself. That's one of the things wrong with history". We need to remember that man is at the wheel of history; history is not in control of man. The *Plessy v. Ferguson* case is one that we can learn from. Nonetheless, we still need a script that helps us to avoid the mistakes in the first place. Here the Gospel message, including the commandment to love one another, remains paramount.

The Art of Tact

Tact is a way of making a point without making an enemy. It is correcting a friend without bruising his ego. And we all know, or at least should know, how fragile the ego can be. Tact is being sensitive to other people's sensitivities.

We need to be tactful so that our friends, relatives, colleagues, or associates do not remain in error. Tact is the delicate art that involves the proper balancing of respect, support, council, correction, and even kindness. "The greatest kindness one can render to any man," wrote Saint Thomas Aquinas, "consists in leading him to truth." The transition from error to truth, however, is often stubbornly resisted. People, as a rule, would rather save face than face the music.

Tact, therefore, is a rescue mission, delivering a person from the darkness of error to the light of truth. Poor John Wesley, the founder of Methodism, had to abide his wife, Molly Vazeille's heckling while he preached. Shakespeare's *Taming of the Shrew* is a conversion story that offers valuable lessons for many married couples. Xanthippe had the reputation for being an inveterate nag. Once, according to the legend, after severely berating her husband, Socrates, she poured water over his head. "After thunder comes rain," was the Gadfly of Athens' philosophical response.

According to the Bible, "A good woman is hard to find, and worth far more than diamonds. Her husband trusts her without reserve and never has reason to regret it. Never spiteful, she treats him generously all her life long" (*Proverbs* 31).

Hubert Horatio Humphrey, Jr. appeared to have the kind of wife described in Scripture. On one occasion, in 1968, while campaigning for the presidential candidacy, he was talking on and on to the boredom and exasperation of his audience. His wife, Muriel, aware of the problem, sent a note up to the podium. "Dear," she has written, "Remember that for a speech to be immortal it need not be eternal." Thus, she made his immortal words secure. Prefacing her message with the word "dear" established a loving context within which her point would be similarly received – love responding to love. The touch of humor, along with evident intelligence, no doubt got her point across without alienating her husband. A less supportive wife might have said, "Hey, motor-mouth, you are boring your audience to death, shut-up already".

In another instance, after partying at a posh restaurant where Humphrey was lionized as the "bright, new liberal Senator", Muriel questioned her husband as they drove home. "You have to make a choice," she said. "You can turn into a social butterfly, a Washington phony, or you can skip this sort of evening and become a good Senator. You have the choice." Humphrey chose the latter. A tactful wife can be a great blessing.

HHH was not without humor of his own: "Behind every successful man is a proud wife and a surprised mother-in-law." Nor was he bereft of moral wisdom: "It was once said that the moral test of government is how that government treats those who are in the dawn of life, the children, those who are in the twilight of life, the elderly, and those who are in the shadows of life, the sick, the needy, and the handicapped."

In the *Book of Samuel*, Elkanah was a model of tactfulness toward his wife who was depressed because she had not given birth. "Hannah," he said to his wife, "why weepest thou? And why eatest thou not? And why is thy heart grieved? Am I not better to thee than ten sons?" Elkanah's love and patience with Hannah and the attention he lavished on her was beautiful to behold. A less loving husband might have simply said, "Snap out of it". Elkanah's tactfulness proved beneficial. Hannah gave birth to a boy and named him Samuel.

Communication is greatly facilitated when it is established in a ground of communion. We live in a society in which communication abounds in many forms. We are technical geniuses when it comes to passing on information, but information that is not founded in communion is easily rejected or misinterpreted. A parent's word to a child has more impact than the most cleverly packaged bit of information that comes through the airways. One Television news service boasts that it is the "most trusted" of its kind, largely because it is not trusted.

Existential philosopher Gabriel Marcel drew attention to the fact than we can feel alienated from the person sitting next us even though we can understand what he is saying. "One might say," according to Marcel, "that what we have with this person, who is in the room, but somehow not really present to us, is communication without communion." Marcel popularized the notion of *presence* to describe the sense that, in some mysterious way, I can be in communion with another human being and am not a stranger to him.

The American comedy film *Lovers and Other Strangers*, is typical of the many Hollywood characterizations of marriage that involve spouses who are not present to each other. In the absence of this "presence," this mutual regard, they are unable to communicate with each other and, as a result, drift apart. The language of *our* needs to replace the dichotomy of *you* and *me*.

Tact, at its best, is expressed between people who are present to each other. To be an object for another object is to lack this presence. Tactfulness is neither an order nor a command. It requires a certain empathy and ministers with a gentle hand. It is uplifting and never insulting. Human relationships would enjoy a quantum leap of improvement if this delicate art could be employed more frequently.

The Advantage of Wit

Washington and Lincoln stand as America's most prominent heroes. Therefore, writes journalist George H. Smythe, Jr., "Our nation has most rightly and fittingly made the birthdays of these, her illustrious sons, legal holidays, to inspire us to a purer, nobler, holier manhood". These words, once echoed by many, no longer seem right and fitting. The birthdays of these two illustrious presidents have been absorbed into Presidents' Day, which in turn, has been overshadowed by using February as an opportunity to advertise car sales. Removing the spotlight from Washington and Lincoln is a grave misfortune at a time when both political greatness and unswerving patriotism are either disputed or are no longer in fashion. Washington and Lincoln are now rendered virtually anonymous, their distinctive contributions to America overshadowed by a number of presidents who were decidedly mediocre.

I want to take this opportunity to celebrate the illuminating wit of Abraham Lincoln. Wit may be contrasted with humor. Lincoln's wit rose above the pedestrian notion of humor. It had a moral point to it. It included humor, but illuminated a moral issue in a way that was both disarming as well as revealing. In addition, Lincoln possessed a *ready* wit which he could summon in an impromptu fashion. These abilities made him a formidable debater.

Lincoln's wit was abundantly evident in his debates against slavery advocate Senator Stephen A. Douglas, one of the most skillful debaters at that time in Congress. Douglas had great respect for Lincoln and did not take his debating skills lightly. "I shall have my hands full," he told a Philadelphia journalist. "He is the strong man of his party—full of wit, facts, dates, and the best stump-speaker, with his droll ways and dry jokes, in the West. He is honest as he is shrewd; and if I beat him, my victory will be hard won." Douglas did not enter the debates with Lincoln—there were seven of them—overconfident.

In one exchange, Lincoln said that the argument that Douglas puts forth in defense of slavery is "as thin as the homeopathic soup that is made by boiling the shadow of a pigeon that had been starved to death". On another occasion Lincoln drew from his youthful experiences along the Sangamon River. He made reference to an old steamboat on that river whose boiler was so weak that when it blew the whistle, the paddle could not turn, and when the paddle turned, there was not enough force to blow the whistle. He related this image to "My friend Douglas . . . for it is evident that when he talks he can't think, and when he thinks, he can't talk".

Throughout the debates, Douglas frequently made reference to Lincoln's lowly station in life. In one of his speeches he told his audience that the first time he met Lincoln was across the counter in a general store where his adversary was selling whiskey. Knowing that there were many temperate people among his listeners, Douglas padded his point by asserting, "And an excellent bartender he was, too." Lincoln would not be outshone. When the laughter finally died down, Lincoln, a teetotaler, rose to the occasion. It was a perfect opportunity for exercising his ready wit. "What Mr. Douglas says is quite true. I did keep a general store and sold cotton and candies and cigars and sometimes whiskey, and I particularly remember Mr. Douglas, as he was a very good customer. Many a time I have been on the one side of the counter and sold whiskey to Mr. Douglas on the other side. But now there's a difference between us: I've left my side of the counter, but he sticks to his as tenaciously as ever." Douglas had been forewarned; now it was time for him to sample some rich humble pie.

Lincoln also respected the old adage that brevity is the soul of wit. Concerning slavery, he said, "Whenever I hear anyone arguing for slavery, I feel a strong impulse to see it tried on him personally". On psychology, he stated that "Character is like a tree and reputation like a shadow. The shadow is what we think of it; the tree is the real thing". On the subject of theology, he had this to say: "Sir, my concern is not whether God is on our side, my greatest concern is to be on God's side, for God is always right". On marriage, he quipped, "Marriage is neither heaven nor hell; it is simply purgatory". About personal development, he advised, "You have to do your own growing no matter how tall your grandfather was". Finally, about his own life, he told us, "I pass my life in preventing the storm from blowing down the tent, and I drive the pegs as fast as they are pulled up".

Wit is the felicitous combination of humor and insight. The humor disarms, while the insight enlightens. Lincoln possessed wit in this sense to an extraordinary degree. It served him well both as a human being and as a political leader.

We often depict our 16th president in a somewhat stereotypical way. He is the tall, lanky figure with a stove pipe hat atop a furrowed countenance partly obscured by poorly groomed facial hair. He is, of course, far more than that, though he could laugh at himself: "There are no bad pictures; that's how you face looks sometimes". He certainly had cause to worry. Yet, by virtue of his brilliant mind and an illuminating wit, he was able to endure, and even transcend the various trials that came his way. During the month of February, his birth month, we should pay special tribute to this great human being, pathfinder, and incomparable patriot.

About the Author

Dr. Donald DeMarco is Prof. Emeritus/St. Jerome's University, Adjunct Prof./Holy Apostles College & Seminary. He is a regular columnist for the *St. Austin Review.* His latest two books, *How To Navigate through Life* and *Apostles of the Culture of Life,* are posted on amazon.com .

9 789997 534029